Foundations *of our* Faith & Calling

Foundations

of our Faith *&* Calling

THE BRUDERHOF

THE PLOUGH PUBLISHING HOUSE

Published by The Plough Publishing House
Rifton, New York
Robertsbridge, England

17 16 15 14 13 12   2 3 4 5 6 7 8

Scripture quotations are from the Revised Standard Version of the Bible (1971) except as indicated by reference to the New Revised Standard Version (1989), New International Version (2011), or English Standard Version (2011).

The ecumenical translation of the Apostles' Creed opposite page 1 is from the English Language Liturgical Consultation (1988).

References to early Christian writers (ca. AD 60–150) follow the 2007 edition of *The Apostolic Fathers,* ed. Michael W. Holmes.

Library of Congress Cataloging-in-Publication Data

Foundations of our faith and calling / The Bruderhof
    p. cm.
  ISBN-13: 978-0-87486-888-3 (hardcover)
  ISBN-10: 0-87486-888-2 (hardcover)
  ISBN-13: 978-0-87486-889-0 (pbk.)
  ISBN-10: 0-87486-889-0 (pbk.)
1. Bruderhof Communities.
  BX8129.B65F68 2012
  230'.73--dc23
                        2012025464

Printed in the United States of America

CONTENTS

Introductory Note

From the New Testament church onward, Christians have testified to their faith through the written word. Following in that tradition the members of the Bruderhof, a Christian church community founded in 1920, have published *Foundations of Our Faith and Calling:*

1. as a public account of the faith and life we share together; and

2. as a statement of the foundations and orders common to all Bruderhof communities throughout the world.

Foundations is the outcome of discussion and study within the Bruderhof communities about the basis of our life together. The members took active part in drafting the text, providing comments, criticisms, and suggestions as the document gradually took shape. This period of reflection concluded with a meeting of all Bruderhof members worldwide on June 24, 2012, in which the members unanimously adopted the final text that appears here.

Since the members intend *Foundations* to remain a living document, it may be amended in the same way as it was adopted. ✝

The Apostles' Creed

I believe in God, the Father almighty,
  creator of heaven and earth.

I believe in Jesus Christ, God's only Son, our Lord,
  who was conceived by the Holy Spirit,
  born of the Virgin Mary,
  suffered under Pontius Pilate,
  was crucified, died, and was buried;
  he descended to the dead.
  On the third day he rose again;
  he ascended into heaven,
  he is seated at the right hand of the Father,
  and he will come to judge the living and the dead.

I believe in the Holy Spirit,
  the holy catholic Church,
  the communion of saints,
  the forgiveness of sins,
  the resurrection of the body,
  and the life everlasting.

Amen.

I

BASIS OF OUR FAITH

1.   Our life together is founded on Jesus, the Christ and son of God. We desire to love him, to follow him, to obey his commandments, and to testify in word and deed to the coming of his kingdom here on earth.

John 1:1–14; 14:6; Col 1:15–20
1 Cor 3:11; Luke 6:47–49
John 14:15; Rom 10:8–15
Matt 6:9–10

2.   Our faith is grounded in the Bible, the authoritative witness to the living Word of God. Through the Holy Spirit, we seek to be guided in all things by the New and Old Testaments.

2 Tim 3:14–17
Matt 5:17–19; Is 55:10–11
Luke 24:25–47; 2 Pet 1:19–21
Deut 6:4–9

3.   We hold to the teaching and example of the early Christians and affirm the apostolic rule of faith in the triune God as stated in the Apostles' and Nicene Creeds.

Acts 2:42–47
Eph 2:19–20
Matt 28:19

4.   We stem from the Anabaptist tradition, but feel akin to all who are pledged to full discipleship of Jesus. We recognize his power to work in all people, regardless of their creed or walk of life.

1 Jn 2:5–6
John 1:9; 10:16
Acts 17:24–28; Ps 67

2

OUR CALLING

The Kingdom of God

5   Our calling is to Jesus, who calls all people to himself.   *Acts 4:11–12; John 12:32*

Jesus brought the good news of the kingdom of God: *Matt 4:17, 23*
"The time is fulfilled, and the kingdom of God is at   *Mark 1:15*
hand; repent, and believe in the gospel." What is this
kingdom? It is where God's whole will is done, his   *Matt 6:10; Ps 103:19–22*
justice is upheld, and his domain of peace has become   *Ps 9:7–8; Is 9:6–7; 42:2–4*
reality as Israel's prophets foretold. Jesus sums up the   *Jer 23:5–6; Is 11:6–9; Mic 4:1–5*
nature of the kingdom in two great commandments:
"Love the Lord your God with all your heart, and with   *Mark 12:30–31*
all your soul, and with all your mind, and with all your   *Deut 6:4–5*
strength," and "Love your neighbor as yourself."   *Lev 19:16–18*

Jesus asks us to live as citizens of his coming kingdom.   *John 3:3–5; Matt 5:19–20*
It is not enough to accept him as our personal savior
or to say to him "Lord, Lord." We must prove our love   *Matt 7:21; 21:28–32*
to him in deeds, putting into practice his words in the   *John 15:9–17; Jas 1:22–25*
Gospels, especially the Sermon on the Mount. We do   *Matt 5—7; Luke 6:17–49*

From the Sermon on the Mount

Seeing the crowds, he went up on the mountain, and when he sat down his disciples came to him. And he opened his mouth and taught them, saying:

Blessed are the poor in spirit,
   for theirs is the kingdom of heaven.

Blessed are those who mourn, for they shall be comforted.

Blessed are the meek, for they shall inherit the earth.

Blessed are those who hunger and thirst for righteousness,
   for they shall be satisfied.

Blessed are the merciful, for they shall obtain mercy.

Blessed are the pure in heart, for they shall see God.

Blessed are the peacemakers,
   for they shall be called sons of God.

Blessed are those who are persecuted for righteousness' sake,
   for theirs is the kingdom of heaven.

Blessed are you when men revile you and persecute you and utter all kinds of evil against you falsely on my account. Rejoice and be glad, for your reward is great in heaven, for so men persecuted the prophets who were before you.

Matthew 5:1–12

not want a religion that seeks the future of humanity
only beyond this earth and pacifies people with mere
spirituality. No, we and all humankind need to receive   *John 10:10*
help here and now. Jesus seeks to transform the entirety   *2 Cor 10:5*
of our world, including the economic, the social, and   *Matt 28:18*
all other aspects of life. His commands are practical: *John 14:23–24*
to forgive unconditionally; to renounce all violence;
to stay faithful in lifelong marriage; to live free from
wealth; to serve as the least and lowest; and to give up
all power over others. His teaching is not an impossible   *Luke 18:26–30*
ideal, but is truly good news: the news that the despair
and death that rule the present age can be overcome   *Luke 7:18–23*
through a life lived according to perfect love.   *1 Jn 2:5–11*

It is Jesus himself who brings this about. In him, the   *Luke 4:17–21*
Messiah, God's reign has already begun on earth,   *Matt 1:1–17; John 1:35–51*
and when he comes again he will establish it fully,
redeeming all creation. He promises: "Behold, I make   *Rom 8:18–25; Rev 21:5*
all things new."   *Is 65:17–25*

Church Community

6 To live for the kingdom of God leads to church   *1 Jn 4:20–21*
community. God wants to gather a people on earth   *Luke 13:34–35; Gen 12:1–3*
who belong to his new creation. He calls them out to   *Is 42:6–7; 60:1–3*
form a new society that makes his justice and peace   *2 Cor 3:5–6; 5:17–21*
tangible. Among them private property falls away, and   *Luke 6:34–38*
they are united in a bond of solidarity and equality   *2 Cor 8:13–15*
in which each one says: Whatever I have belongs to   *1 Jn 3:16–17; Deut 15:4–8*
the others, and if I am ever in need, they will help me.
Then Jesus' words can come true: "Do not be anxious,   *Matt 6:31–33*

5

From the Book of Acts

They *hey devoted themselves to the apostles' teaching and fellowship, to the breaking of bread and the prayers. And fear came upon every soul; and many wonders and signs were done through the apostles. And all who believed were together and had all things in common; and they sold their possessions and goods and distributed them to all, as any had need. And day by day, attending the temple together and breaking bread in their homes, they partook of food with glad and generous hearts, praising God and having favor with all the people. And the Lord added to their number day by day those who were being saved.*

Now *ow the company of those who believed were of one heart and soul, and no one said that any of the things which he possessed was his own, but they had everything in common. And with great power the apostles gave their testimony to the resurrection of the Lord Jesus, and great grace was upon them all. There was not a needy person among them, for as many as were possessors of lands or houses sold them, and brought the proceeds of what was sold and laid it at the apostles' feet; and distribution was made to each as any had need.*

Acts 2:42–47; 4:32–35

saying, 'What shall we eat?' or 'What shall we drink?' or 'What shall we wear?' For the Gentiles seek all these things; and your heavenly Father knows that you need them all. But seek first his kingdom and his righteousness, and all these things shall be yours as well."

Such a people came into being in Jerusalem at the first Pentecost. As described in Acts 2 and 4, the Holy Spirit descended on the believers who had gathered after Jesus' resurrection, and the first communal church was born. Just as it was then, so it will be today whenever *Acts 2:38–39; Joel 2:28–32* the Spirit is poured out on a group of people. They will *Ezek 36:24—37:28* be filled with love for Christ and for one another, and their communion of love will lead them to share their goods, talents, and lives, boldly testifying to the gospel. *Acts 4:31* This is our calling in church community.

We are a fellowship of brothers and sisters, both single and married, who are called by Christ to follow him *John 15:16* together in a common life in the spirit of the first church in Jerusalem. We desire to remain true to this *Eph 4:1–3* calling all our lives. For its sake we gladly renounce all *Mark 10:28–31; Phil 3:12–16* private property, personal claims, and worldly attach- *Luke 9:57–62; 1 Jn 2:15–17* ments and honors. Our vocation is a life of service to *Matt 22:37–40* God and humankind, freely giving our whole working *Rom 13:8–10; Gal 5:13–14* strength and all that we have and are.

7   Church community is a gift of the Holy Spirit. Any *Acts 2:4, 39–47* attempt to force it into being will produce only a *Ps 127:1–2* disappointing caricature. Without help from above, we human beings are selfish and divided, unfit for life *Rom 7:14–25*

John 15:5

Eph 2:8–10

together. Our best motives and efforts ultimately prove unsound; as Jesus tells us, "Apart from me you can do nothing." We remain sinners utterly dependent on grace.

2 Cor 5:14–17; Gal 2:20

Phil 4:13

John 6:63–65

John 17:18–23

Yet we have experienced Christ's transforming love. He makes the impossible possible: for ordinary men and women to live together in forgiveness and mutual trust, as brothers and sisters, the children of one Father. It is his Spirit that calls believers to a life of love where work, worship, mission, education, and family life are brought together into a single whole. We are convinced that such a life in church community is the greatest service we can render humanity and the best way we can proclaim Christ.

Rom 5:6–11

John 1:29; Is 52:13—53:12

John 3:16; 1 Jn 2:2

Eph 1:7–10; 2:11–22

Heb 10:11–25

Col 1:19–20; 2:13–15

8 Christ brings all this about through his sacrifice on the cross. By taking suffering and death upon himself, he atoned for our sins and the sins of the whole world. His cross is the only place we can be forgiven and find peace with God and one another. The cross is the means of our personal salvation, but it is also more: it has cosmic significance. Here Christ overcomes all powers of evil and enmity, fulfills the justice of God, and reconciles the whole universe to himself.

1 Cor 1:18–25

Mark 8:34

Christ's cross is at the center of our life together. "If any man would come after me, let him deny himself and take up his cross and follow me." We seek to go

8

the way of the cross as he did – the way of humility, *Mark 10:42–45*
vulnerability, and self-sacrificing love. *Phil 2:1–11*

9 Our church community is only a small part of the
universal church. This universal church is the body *Matt 16:18; Eph 4:4–6*
of Christ, made up of all who belong to him; it is his *1 Cor 12:12–13; Eph 5:25–27*
bride, set apart for him alone. It cannot be identified *Rev 21:1–14; Hos 2:19–20*
with any human institution or group. As the early
Christians testify,* it is a work of God, not of man.
Ordained from the beginning of creation, it includes *Rev 7:9–10*
the apostles, prophets, martyrs, and believers from
every age who are with God as the "cloud of witnesses" *Heb 12:1–2, 22–24*
from every nation, tribe, and race. *Rev 5:9–10*

If asked whether we are the one true church, we reply,
"No" – we are merely objects of God's mercy like
everybody else. But if asked whether we experience
the church as a reality in our daily lives, then we must
affirm that we do, through the grace of God. Jesus
promises that wherever even two or three are gathered *Matt 18:18–20*
in his name – that is, in full love and obedience to *Matt 28:19–20*
him – he will be present in their midst. Then their
fellowship will be united with the one holy, universal, *Gal 3:26–29*
and apostolic church.

Christ is the head of this church. Just as a single vine *Eph 1:22–23; John 15:1–8*
nourishes many branches, so he joins together the
diverse bands of his followers on earth, endowing *John 20:21–23*
them with his authority, unity, and commission. *Matt 16:19*

---

* *The Shepherd of Hermas,* 3.4, 8.1 (ca. AD 95–154).

From the Sermon on the Mount

You have heard that it was said to the men of old, "You shall not kill; and whoever kills shall be liable to judgment." But I say to you that every one who is angry with his brother shall be liable to judgment; whoever insults his brother shall be liable to the council, and whoever says, "You fool!" shall be liable to the hell of fire.

You have heard that it was said, "An eye for an eye and a tooth for a tooth." But I say to you, Do not resist one who is evil. But if any one strikes you on the right cheek, turn to him the other also; and if any one would sue you and take your coat, let him have your cloak as well; and if any one forces you to go one mile, go with him two miles. Give to him who begs from you, and do not refuse him who would borrow from you.

You have heard that it was said, "You shall love your neighbor and hate your enemy." But I say to you, Love your enemies and pray for those who persecute you, so that you may be sons of your Father who is in heaven; for he makes his sun rise on the evil and on the good, and sends rain on the just and on the unjust. For if you love those who love you, what reward have you? Do not even the tax collectors do the same? And if you salute only your brethren, what more are you doing than others? Do not even the Gentiles do the same? You, therefore, must be perfect, as your heavenly Father is perfect.

Matthew 5:21–22, 38–48

The Way of Peace

10 Peace is the very nature of the kingdom of God; Christ entrusted his church with the gospel of peace. "Peace I leave with you; my peace I give to you." He himself is our peace, and in him all division is overcome. He wants us to be makers of his peace.

Is 9:6–7; Ps 85:8–13; Rom 14:17
Acts 10:34–38; Eph 6:14–15
John 14:27
Eph 2:14–18; Mic 5:4–5
Matt 5:9; Ps 34:11–14

For this purpose, he assigns us to be in the world, but not of the world. We must not be conformed to the present world, which has fallen subject to sin and death, powers that are at enmity with God. But neither are we to despise it.

John 15:18–19; 17:14–18
Rom 12:2

John 3:17; 12:47

"God so loved the world...." Christ calls us to the same love. In his service, we cannot withdraw or cloister ourselves. He asks us to be the city on the hill, the light on the lampstand, and the salt of the earth. His church is to be the embassy of his kingdom of peace, stationed in the present age as in a foreign jurisdiction.

John 3:16; Matt 5:43–48
Col 2:20–23; Jer 29:7
Matt 5:13–16

2 Cor 5:18–20
Heb 13:14; 1 Pet 2:9–11

We seek to fulfill this calling by working together with others of goodwill, whether or not they are confessing believers. In our experience, Christ can work even in people who deny him with their lips. Our task is to recognize him in each person and to point all people to him.

Mark 9:38–41
Heb 11:31; Josh 2
Is 44:24—45:7
Matt 21:28–32; 25:31–46
John 1:9; Matt 8:5–13

11 What does it mean to be peacemakers? Jesus instructed us: Love your enemies, do good to those who hate you, pray for those who persecute you, and forgive as you need to be forgiven. He taught: Do not resist those

Matt 5:38–48; Exod 23:4–5
Matt 18:21–35
Luke 6:27–36

who mistreat you, but allow yourself to be struck again rather than to strike back. He rejected political power when it was offered to him, and he refused to defend himself with force, rather letting himself be killed. We must do the same.

Luke 4:5–8

John 18:36

1 Pet 2:20–25

The way of peace demands reverence for all life, above all each human life, since every person is made in the image of God. Christ's word and example, as affirmed by the teaching of the early church, absolutely forbid us to take human life for any reason, directly or indirectly, whether in war or self-defense, through the death penalty, or by any other means, including euthanasia or abortion.* As conscientious objectors, we will not serve in the armed services of any country, not even as noncombatants. Nor may we support war-making or the use of deadly force by others through our consent or aid.

Gen 1:26–27; 9:5–6

Matt 26:50–54

Rom 13:9–10

2 Cor 10:3–4

Jas 3:18

1 Thess 5:15

We refuse to wield governmental power by serving in high office or in any position such as judge or juror that is vested with power over the life, liberty, or civil rights of another.† Likewise, in obedience to Christ's teaching, we cannot swear oaths or make any pledge of allegiance. We love our country and our countrymen, but equally we love all our fellow human beings regardless of their nationality, ancestry, race, creed, culture, or social status. Our loyalty is to the kingdom of God.

Luke 12:13–14

Matt 5:33–37

Jas 5:12

Jas 2:1–13

Gal 3:28

Phil 3:20

---

* See for example *Didache,* 1.1–4, 2.2, 3.2 (ca. AD 60–110); Athenagoras of Athens, *Legatio,* Chapter 35 (ca. AD 176–180).

† Peter Walpot, "Article 4: Concerning the Sword," in *The Great Article Book* (*Großes Artikelbuch,* ca. 1577).

12 In regard to government, Jesus teaches: "Give back to Caesar what is Caesar's and to God what is God's." We respect the authority of the state as appointed by God to protect the innocent and to restrain evil. We pay our taxes and obey the laws of the land, so long as these do not conflict with obedience to Christ. We acknowledge the state's legitimate efforts to check murder, dishonesty, and immorality, and we pray for our government leaders to use their authority to promote peace and justice.

Mark 12:17 NIV

John 19:11; Dan 2:21

Rom 13:1–7

Titus 3:1–2

1 Pet 2:13–16

1 Tim 2:1–4

Yet we can never give the state our allegiance, since "we must obey God rather than men." As Christ teaches and history shows, the church must stay disentangled from the state to avoid being corrupted by it. The power of the state is ultimately the power of the sword, secured by violence. We, however, are called to the way of Christ, which overcomes evil with good.

Acts 5:29; Dan 3:16–18

Mark 10:42–45

Rom 13:4; Rev 13

1 Sam 8

Rom 12:17–21; 13:8

Even so, we are not indifferent to the work of government. At its best, the state represents a relative order of justice in the present sinful world; but the church, as God's embassy, represents an absolute order of justice: the righteousness of the kingdom of God.* The church must witness to the state, serving as its conscience, helping it to distinguish good from evil, and reminding it not to overstep the bounds of its God-appointed authority.

1 Pet 2:17

John 17:15–19; 2 Cor 5:17–20

1 Kgs 18:1–19

Acts 4:18–20; 22:22–29

Matt 14:1–12

---

* Eberhard Arnold, *God's Revolution* (talks and writings 1915–1935; published 1984).

13 We uphold the way of nonviolent love and unconditional forgiveness. This is not a pacifism of detachment or cowardice. Jesus calls us to be ambassadors of peace, even at the risk of death or dishonor. Opposing war is only the first step; we seek to build up a life that removes the occasion for war by overcoming its root causes: injustice, hatred, and greed. We want to use our lives to advance the peaceable kingdom foretold by the prophets, which will transform not only individuals but also all human society and the whole of nature:

Matt 6:14–15

Heb 10:32–39

Jas 3:13—4:12

Mic 4:1–5

Is 65:17–25; Hos 2:18

Is 11:6, 9

> The wolf shall dwell with the lamb,
> and the leopard shall lie down with the kid,
> and the calf and the lion and the fatling together,
> and a little child shall lead them.
>
> They shall not hurt or destroy
> in all my holy mountain;
> for the earth shall be full of the knowledge
>   of the Lord
> as the waters cover the sea.

Justice and the Works of Mercy

14 To work for God's peaceable kingdom means to strive for his justice. What does this justice demand of us? It demands that we put love of God and love of neighbor into practice.

Matt 6:33; Is 42:1–4

Is 58; Mic 6:6–8

1 Jn 4:19–21

Luke 10:25–37

15 Love of neighbor means a life wholly dedicated to service. This is the opposite of all selfish pursuits, including a focus on one's personal salvation. We

John 13:12–17; Gal 5:13

Gal 6:9–10

1 Cor 13:1–3

14

live in church community because we must concern
ourselves with the need of the whole world. We *John 1:29; 3:16–17*
each acknowledge our share in humanity's guilt and *Rom 3:9, 23*
suffering, and we must respond through a life devoted *Rom 13:8–10; Gal 5:6*
to love. "Whatever you wish that men would do to you, *Matt 7:12*
do so to them; for this is the law and the prophets."

16 Love of neighbor means doing the works of mercy *Matt 25:31–46*
commanded by Christ: giving food to the hungry and
water to the thirsty, welcoming the stranger, clothing
the naked, giving alms to the poor, and visiting the sick *Deut 15:1–11; 24:10–22*
and those in prison. "Truly, I say to you, as you did it to *Matt 25:40*
one of the least of these my brethren, you did it to me."
Like the early Christians, we see piety as false unless it *Jas 1:27*
is proved authentic through deeds of social justice. *Deut 10:12–21; Ps 112*

17 Love of neighbor means that we keep an open *Heb 13:2*
door. The blessings of a life of brotherly and sisterly *Lev 19:33–34*
community are available to all people, rich or poor, *Col 3:11; 1 Cor 14:23–25*
skilled or unskilled, who are called to go this way of
discipleship with us.

18 Love of neighbor leads us to give up all private *Luke 12:32–34*
property, the root of so much injustice and violence. *Jas 4:1–4; 1 Tim 6:9–10*
Christ teaches his followers to reject mammon – the *Matt 6:19–21, 24*
desire for and the power of possessions. He warns,
"How difficult it is for those who have wealth to enter *Luke 18:24 ESV*
the kingdom of God!" He saw into the heart of the
rich young man whom he loved and told him: "You *Mark 10:17–22 ESV*
lack one thing: go, sell all that you have and give to the

From the Sermon on the Mount

Do not lay up for yourselves treasures on earth, where moth and rust consume and where thieves break in and steal, but lay up for yourselves treasures in heaven, where neither moth nor rust consumes and where thieves do not break in and steal. For where your treasure is, there will your heart be also.

No one can serve two masters; for either he will hate the one and love the other, or he will be devoted to the one and despise the other. You cannot serve God and mammon.

Therefore I tell you, do not be anxious about your life, what you shall eat or what you shall drink, nor about your body, what you shall put on. Is not life more than food, and the body more than clothing? Look at the birds of the air: they neither sow nor reap nor gather into barns, and yet your heavenly Father feeds them. Are you not of more value than they?...And why are you anxious about clothing? Consider the lilies of the field, how they grow; they neither toil nor spin; yet I tell you, even Solomon in all his glory was not arrayed like one of these....

Therefore do not be anxious, saying, "What shall we eat?" or "What shall we drink?" or "What shall we wear?" For the Gentiles seek all these things; and your heavenly Father knows that you need them all. But seek first his kingdom and his righteousness, and all these things shall be yours as well.

Matthew 6:19–21, 24–33

poor, and you will have treasure in heaven; and come, follow me."

Mammon is the enemy of love. It drives some to build up individual fortunes while millions lead lives of misery. As a force within economic systems, it breeds exploitation, fraud, materialism, injustice, and war.

Jas 5:1–6; 1 Jn 2:15–17

Jer 22:13–17

Ezek 28:1–19; Rev 18

Amos 5:11–24

All that serves mammon opposes the rule of God. A person who keeps anything for himself disregards Jesus' commandment to his followers to give up their private property. He has taken something intended by God for the use of all and claimed it for himself.

Matt 5:42

1 Jn 3:16–18

Luke 12:13–34

Exod 16:13–21

Luke 6:24–36; 16:19–31

In obedience to Christ, we trust in God for everything, including our material needs. None of us owns anything personally, and our communal property belongs not to us as a group but to the cause of Christ in church community.* In this, we follow the example of Christ and his itinerant community of disciples, who kept a common purse.

Matt 6:25–34; Exod 16

Acts 4:32

John 12:6; 13:29

19 Love of neighbor demands that we stand with the mistreated, the voiceless, and the oppressed. We are bound to confront public and private wrong boldly with the authority of the gospel, just as Jesus did. He himself was born in poverty and died the death of a criminal. His kingdom is especially for the poor and lowly, and he promises that when he returns, the last will be first and the first will be last.

Is 58:6–10; Prov 14:31; 19:17

Pss 72:1–4; 146:1–10

Luke 13:31–32

Matt 23:13–36

Luke 1:46–55

Mark 10:31

---

* Peter Walpot, "Article 3: True Surrender and Christian Community of Goods," in *The Great Article Book* (*Großes Artikelbuch*, ca. 1577).

Luke 4:18–19 ESV   Jesus declares: "The Spirit of the Lord is upon me,

Is 61:1–4   because he has anointed me to proclaim good news
to the poor. He has sent me to proclaim liberty to the
captives and recovering of sight to the blind, to set at
liberty those who are oppressed, to proclaim the year of
the Lord's favor." We are called to help him in his work

Matt 12:20; Is 42:1–4   of redemption, bringing justice to victory.

Proclaiming the Gospel

Mark 16:15–18   **20** After his resurrection, Jesus commissioned his disciples

Matt 28:18–20   to announce the gospel of the kingdom: "All authority
in heaven and on earth has been given to me. Go there-
fore and make disciples of all nations, baptizing them
in the name of the Father and of the Son and of the
Holy Spirit, teaching them to observe all that I have
commanded you; and lo, I am with you always, to the
close of the age."

21 As often as possible, the church community sends
out brothers and sisters to proclaim the gospel. In

Matt 9:35–38   doing so, our prayer is that the original apostolic

Acts 5:12–16; 8:4–8   commission might become a reality today as it was in

Acts 10:44–48; 19:11–12   New Testament times: for Christ's messengers to be

Mark 6:7–13; Luke 9:1–6   equipped with the full authority of the Spirit, going

Luke 14:23   into all the world to invite people to the great feast of
the kingdom of God. We pray that God grants this
gift somewhere, whether to us or to others. But what-

John 17:18; 20:21–23   ever the measure of grace he gives us, he sends us out as

2 Cor 5:16–20   envoys of his kingdom, and we desire to obey.

The gospel we proclaim is alive and gives life: "Man shall not live by bread alone, but by every word that proceeds from the mouth of God." Ours is not a silent God. His Word is not cast in iron or set in the dead letters of holy books. The Word of God is Christ himself, his presence and his power. This living Word never contradicts the Bible, which testifies to him and his will, but is spoken again and again by the Spirit into human hearts.* He opens our eyes to the meaning of Scripture and teaches us everything we must do.

John 10:10

Matt 4:4

Heb 1:1–2

2 Cor 3:1–6; Is 55:10–11

John 1:1–4; Rev 19:11–16

Heb 4:12; Jer 23:29

Deut 30:11–14; Ps 33:6

1 Cor 2:10–16

Luke 24:25–32

John 14:26; 16:12–15

Those who go out to spread the good news must be sent in the name of Christ by a church community united in a spirit of repentance and love. They must trace the footsteps of Christ as they lead from one person to another and follow them from house to house and town to town. To the extent that we are given discernment to do this, we will find ourselves where he has already gone, among people whose hearts have already been opened by him. Our task is not to proselytize or judge others, but to witness to the greatness of God's kingdom.

Acts 13:1–3

Rom 10:8–15

John 10:16

Acts 8:26–40; 16:11–15

Acts 10:1–48; 17:10–12

2 Cor 4:1–6

22 So, too, those who remain at home in the church community desire to live in a way that testifies to perfect unity, as a sign to all the world of who Jesus is and what he wills.

Col 3:17; 1 Thess 1:2–10

Acts 4:32; Phil 2:1–11

Eph 4:1–3; Ps 133

---

* Eberhard Arnold, "The Living Word," in *Innerland: A Guide into the Heart and Soul of the Bible* (*Innenland: Ein Wegweiser in die Seele der Bibel,* 1936; published in English 1975).

John 13:34–35

John 17:21–23 ESV

How will the world know that the gospel is true? Jesus taught us that it would be through the love and unity visible among his disciples. On the night before his death, he prayed for them and for all believers who would come after them: "That they may all be one, just as you, Father, are in me, and I in you, that they also may be in us, so that the world may believe that you have sent me. The glory that you have given me I have given to them, that they may be one even as we are one, I in them and you in me, that they may become perfectly one, so that the world may know that you sent me and loved them even as you loved me."

1 Cor 6:19–20

Eph 4:30–32

Matt 5:14–16; Eph 5:8–16

Oneness in Jesus is a great grace. This grace is not cheap. It demands deeds of love and repentance. It requires giving and receiving forgiveness again and again. Yet if we live in the unity that Jesus prayed for, it will shine out into the whole world as a powerful proclamation of his coming kingdom.*

---

* Peter Riedemann, "What the Church Is," in *Account of Our Religion, Doctrine, and Faith* (*Rechenschafft unserer Religion, Leer und Glaubens,* ca. 1540–1542; published in English 1950).

3

HERITAGE

23 Our community is but a small part of what God – the
God of Abraham, Isaac, and Jacob – has done through
the ages. Glimpses of his divine truth have been caught
throughout history by sages, philosophers, and poets;
from early peoples in their reverence for the Creator;
to Socrates, Buddha, and Zoroaster; to visionaries such
as Leo Tolstoy, Albert Schweitzer, and Simone Weil.
Right down to the present, wherever people strive for
truth, justice, brotherhood, and peace, God is at work.
We do not seek to imitate those who have gone before
us; rather, we wish for their example to inspire us to live
more wholeheartedly for God's kingdom.

Heb 1:1–4; 11:1—12:2

Acts 17:24–28

Rom 2:14–16

Matt 25:31–46

Ps 44:1–3; Deut 6:20–25

Rev 14:13

Our Founding
24 Our community was founded in 1920 in Germany by
the Protestant theologian Eberhard Arnold, his wife
Emmy, and her sister Else von Hollander. Appalled

by mounting social injustice and the horrors of
World War I, they sought answers in Jesus' teachings,
especially his Sermon on the Mount. Through this
search they felt a call to radical discipleship: to give up
everything for Christ.* They moved from their Berlin
townhouse to a remote village, Sannerz. There, with
a handful of like-minded seekers, they began to live
in community of goods after the example of the first
church in Jerusalem. Soon they adopted the name
Bruderhof – literally, "place of brothers."

Over the next fifteen years, the community's ranks
swelled with young people from all over Europe,
eventually numbering 150. After Hitler's rise to power
in 1933, however, the community became a target of
National Socialist oppression because of its stand of
conscience. For instance, members refused to use the
Heil Hitler greeting, serve in the German army, or
accept a government teacher in their school. In 1937,
the secret police dissolved the community at gunpoint,
seizing its assets, imprisoning several members, and
giving the rest forty-eight hours to leave.

With the help of Mennonite, Quaker, and Catholic
friends, all members were eventually reunited in
England, and by 1940 the refugee community had
doubled in size through an influx of English members.
Meanwhile, World War II had broken out, and the
British government advised the group either to accept

---

* Emmy Arnold, *Torches Together: The Beginning and Early Years of the
Bruderhof Communities* (published 1964).

the internment of its German nationals or to leave the country. Determined to remain together, almost all members of the community – mostly city-raised Europeans – emigrated to Paraguay. There they spent the next twenty years as pioneer farmers in a harsh, unfamiliar climate, while also founding a hospital that served thousands of local patients. Three members remained in England and soon were building up a new community there as dozens of newcomers continued to arrive.

In 1954, the first American community was founded in Rifton, New York. Today there are Bruderhof communities in the United States, the United Kingdom, Germany, Paraguay, and Australia.

Forerunners

25 We look for our example to the first church founded at Pentecost in Jerusalem.* Here the Spirit worked with unique power, leading Christians to share all they had, to serve the city's poor, and to proclaim the gospel boldly. We believe that this first church community's life and teaching demonstrate what God's will is for humankind.

Acts 2—7

The church in Jerusalem was eventually dispersed through persecution. Yet its spirit could not be quenched. It lived on even after the death of the

---

* Eberhard Arnold, *The Early Christians after the Death of the Apostles* (*Die ersten Christen nach dem Tode der Apostel,* 1926; published in English 1970).

apostles, as attested by the early Christian martyrs. We affirm the early church's rule of faith and we value its witness, including the *Didache* and the writings of church fathers such as Clement of Rome, Hermas, Ignatius, Justin, Tertullian, and Origen.

26 Over the centuries since, the apostolic witness of church community has shone out repeatedly. Though often suppressed or forgotten, it has reemerged again and again in new places and forms. It appeared in the monastic movements from the third century onward – notably among the Desert Fathers, in the community around Augustine of Hippo, and in Celtic Christianity. It appeared in the itinerant Christian communities of the Middle Ages, among the Waldensians, the Beguines and Beghards, and among the followers of Francis of Assisi and Clare of Assisi. It was there among the radical Anabaptists as well as among the early Quakers in the time of George Fox. It was there in the Moravian church of Zinzendorf, and it can be seen in many other movements up to the present day.

In addition to these church communities, the witness of other individual men and women of God is also important to us. These include the medieval mystics Thomas à Kempis and Meister Eckhart in their discipleship of the heart; John Wycliffe and Jan Hus in their courage for the gospel; the early Martin Luther in his experience of undeserved grace; and inspired artists such as Bach and Handel, whose works such as *St. Matthew Passion* and *Messiah* give glory to God. They include the evangelists John Wesley, Charles Finney, Hudson Taylor, and Sadhu Sundar Singh with their zeal for Christ; William and Catherine Booth of the Salvation Army in their care for the poor; Fyodor Dostoevsky in his solidarity with suffering humanity; and Dorothy Day and Mother Teresa with their devotion to the works of mercy. They also include martyrs such as Sophie and Hans Scholl, Dietrich Bonhoeffer, Martin Luther King, Jr., Oscar Romero, and many others who stood up for truth at the cost of their lives.

Guides

27 Three forerunners stand out as defining influences on our communal life and as guides for our future:

28 *The early Hutterian Church.* This communal church arose in central Europe after 1525 when the Anabaptists Felix Manz, Conrad Grebel, and Georg Blaurock set the Radical Reformation in motion by accepting believer's baptism. Soon tens of thousands were following them, despite a bloody campaign of persecution. Unified by the Schleitheim Confession, they championed freedom of conscience and a return to original Christianity in obedience to Jesus' words in *Matt 5—7; 18:15-20* the Gospels, rejecting armed force, infant baptism, and the institutional churches.

One sector of this movement, known as Hutterites after their leader Jakob Hutter, settled in communities, sharing money and possessions, work, housing, and a common daily life founded on brotherly and sisterly love. Zealous to spread the gospel, hundreds suffered martyrdom in the sixteenth and seventeenth centuries.

In the 1920s, the founding members of our community took inspiration from the witness of the early Hutterites, and made contact with their descendants living in North America. In 1930, Eberhard Arnold was ordained as a minister by all branches of the Hutterian church.

At present our community is not affiliated with the Hutterian colonies. We nevertheless seek to live in the same spirit as the original Hutterites during the time of their first love and active mission (1528–1578). We treasure the Hutterian chronicles and spiritual writings – for example, those of Jakob Hutter, Peter Riedemann, Ulrich Stadler, and Peter Walpot.*

29 *The Blumhardts.* Johann Christoph Blumhardt (1805–1880) and his son Christoph Friedrich Blumhardt (1842–1919) were widely known German Lutheran

---

* Caspar Braitmichel et al., *The Chronicle of the Hutterian Brethren,* vol. 1 (*Das große Geschichtbuch der Hutterischen Brüder,* compiled 1565–1665; published in English 1987).

Jakob Hutter, *Brotherly Faithfulness* (letters 1530–1535; published in English 1979).

Peter Riedemann, *Account of Our Religion, Doctrine, and Faith* (*Rechenschafft unserer Religion, Leer und Glaubens,* ca. 1540–1542; published in English 1950).

Ulrich Stadler, "The Living Word" and other writings (ca. 1530–1540; published 1938 in *Glaubenszeugnisse oberdeutscher Taufgesinnter,* vol. 1).

Peter Walpot, *The Great Article Book* (*Großes Artikelbuch,* ca. 1577; Articles 1, 3, and 4 published in English 1992, 1957, and 2009).

pastors. Both men approached all questions of life – whether the personal needs of those they counseled or broader social and political ills – with the conviction that Jesus is victor. They fervently expected that God's kingdom would soon become a reality on earth, bringing redemption not just to an elect few but to all humankind.

Col 2:13–15

Acts 2:17–21

Joel 2:28–32

The Blumhardts' bold attitude of faith and expectation of the kingdom continue to inspire and guide us.*

Rev 21:3–5

30 *The European Youth Movements* (1896–1925). Our community was founded in the midst of a wave of youth movements that swept Germany, Austria, Poland, and Switzerland in the years preceding the rise of National Socialism. Though the young people in these movements held diverse political and religious views, they shared certain common convictions. They rejected materialism and the formalities of social and class-based conventions in favor of genuineness, freedom, equality, and simplicity. They loved hiking, the outdoors, folk culture, and life on the land. Many of them pioneered new approaches to education and work, and – influenced by Jewish philosopher and pacifist Gustav Landauer – saw community as the answer to poverty and social need. By the early 1920s, youth movement ideals were being lived out in more than a hundred communities across Germany, as well as

---

* Friedrich Zündel, *Pastor Johann Christoph Blumhardt* (*Johann Christoph Blumhardt: ein Lebensbild,* 1882; published in English 2010); *Christoph Blumhardt and His Message* (*Christoph Blumhardt und seine Botschaft,* 1938; published in English 1963).

in kibbutzim founded in the Holy Land by the Jewish branches of the movement.

By 1925 the youth movements in Germany were on the wane, and political affiliations were robbing them of their earlier independence. After 1933 they were destroyed by Hitler's regime, which co-opted their energy for its own ends. But their original genuineness and rigor, their emphasis on simplicity and respect for creation, remain essential to our community today.

Rom 12:9; Phil 4:8–9

31 Our particular movement will pass away, but the stream of life to which it belongs can never pass away. We want to remain part of this living stream of God's spirit. This is possible only through an ever new encounter with Christ. As a church community and as individuals, we constantly need times of refreshing through him. God is the Lord of history; as he has ordered the destinies of the nations through the ages, faithfully caring for his covenant people, so he will continue to move and act today. We await his future: the day when he will fulfill all his promises, establishing his kingdom of peace and renewing creation.

Matt 24:35
John 4:23–24

Acts 3:19–21
Deut 32:8; Job 12:13–25

Gen 17:1–8; Deut 7:6–11
Luke 24:44
Num 23:19; 2 Pet 3:9–13
Rev 21:5

4

CHURCH ORDER

32 We want our daily life together to be inspired and led by the Holy Spirit. Order and discipline are fruits of this, for "God is not a God of disorder but of peace." Accordingly, a certain church order has been established in our communities based on Scripture and the example of the early church and shaped by the Anabaptist tradition and our own experience.

John 16:12–13; Eph 5:18–21
Col 2:2–5
1 Cor 14:33 NIV
2 Tim 1:13–14

No system of church order or organization, however good in itself, should ever be allowed to hold back the leading of the spirit of Christ. We belong first and foremost to him. He is the head of the church, and he supersedes all human authorities and traditions. His body is no organization, but a living organism.

1 Cor 2:2–5
Eph 1:22–23
Col 2:8–23
1 Cor 12:12–27; Eph 4:11–16

Becoming a Member

33 Membership in our church community is for life. It is entered into by taking vows. Through our vows,

John 17:20–21; Acts 2:42

29

2 Tim 4:6–7
Deut 6:4–9; 11:13–14
Mark 3:31–35

we give ourselves to Christ with all that we have and are, making a covenant of faithfulness to God and to our fellow members, whom we refer to as brothers and sisters.

2 Pet 1:3–11
Eph 4:1–3

Rom 12:4–5

Lifelong commitment is integral to our vocation: we are convinced that Christ himself has called us to serve him in this particular way with these particular brothers and sisters, come what may. We cannot separate from one another, since "we, though many, are one body in Christ, and individually members one of another." Our promise of faithfulness is what makes mutual trust possible.

Membership is open to all who have received a call to the service of Christ in brotherly and sisterly community and who desire to follow this call with us. In order to take vows, a candidate must have reached the age of twenty-one, understood the teachings of Christ, received believer's baptism and affirmed all points of the Apostles' and Nicene Creeds, and been accepted by the church community after a time of testing and discernment.

1 Jn 4:1

John 21:15–19; Phil 3:7–11

34 Those seeking membership should do so only out of love for Christ. Their vocation will become clear to them only as they obey him in the things of daily life, following him step by step on the way of discipleship.

Luke 9:23–27; Mark 10:21
John 12:24–26
Acts 2:37–41

Full surrender to Christ is the basis of discipleship. This means repentance and conversion, of which baptism is the sign. Anyone who has not yet received believer's baptism – that is, baptism after reaching the age of accountability, as taught in the New Testament – should consider that this is a command of Christ. The church community will recognize a prior baptism performed by another church so long as both we and the person concerned are convinced that the baptism was genuine.

Mark 16:15–16

Matt 28:18–20

35 God wants voluntary service. Vows may be taken only on the basis of a well-tested decision and without any human compulsion. Anyone who cannot make this commitment freely and voluntarily should leave it alone.

1 Pet 5:2; Exod 35:4—36:7

1 Cor 2:4–5

2 Cor 9:6–7; Deut 23:21–23

Gal 5:1

No one should join for the sake of another – a man for the sake of a woman or a woman for the sake of a man, a friend for the sake of a friend, or children for the sake of their parents. Such a decision would be built on sand; it cannot endure. Instead, each one should build on the rock of Christ, seeking to please God alone.

Matt 10:34–39

Matt 7:24–27

Birthright membership is thus out of the question. When young people who have grown up within our communities come of age, they must take time to discern God's will for their lives, either requesting to remain with us or pursuing life experience elsewhere.

John 1:12–13; 3:5–8

No one should join for the sake of personal security. The sixteenth-century Hutterites warned those who came to them: "Each should first count the cost carefully as to what he has to give up....Those who would enter God's service must be prepared to be attacked and

Luke 9:57–58; 2 Cor 6:4–10

Luke 14:26–33

to die for the truth and for the name of Christ, if it be God's will, by water, fire, or the sword. For now we have house and shelter, but we do not know what today or tomorrow will bring. Therefore no one should join for the sake of good days. Rather each must be prepared to endure evil and good with all the believers."*

Matt 5:11–12; John 15:20

1 Pet 4:1

Phil 1:29–30; 2 Tim 3:10–13

36 A person enters into membership in stages:

Guests are welcome among us at the community's discretion, regardless of whether they are interested in membership. Those wishing to remain longer to seek whether God has called them to this way of life can request to stay on as novices. If the church community agrees, and the person concerned is eighteen years of age or older, he or she may be accepted for the novitiate, a time of discernment and testing.

Novices are all those eighteen years of age or older (whether baptized or not) who have requested to take part in the communal life. Novices take part fully in the daily life of the church community, but not in members' meetings. They must respect and uphold the order and spirit of our common life during their stay with us. Their novitiate can be long or short, involves no binding commitment regarding the possibility of membership, and can be broken off by either side at any time.

---

* "Ten Points: What the Church of God Is and How One Is Led into It," church teaching included in the Hutterian baptismal instruction known as the *Taufbüchlein* (ca. 1528–1600).

The novitiate is an opportunity for novices to deepen
their life of faith. Through prayer and through
intellectual and physical work they are to seek the will   *Matt 7:7–11*
of God together with us. Like members, they must
dedicate their talents and working strength to the
church community, having no right to and receiving
no remuneration for their labor or forgone income.
Neither do they have any right to the return of any
property they may contribute. Until accepted into
membership, they retain ownership of any property
not expressly contributed, but they must disclose their
temporal affairs and must make arrangements with the
community for how these are to be managed during
their novitiate.

37 Novices who have become certain of their calling, have
received believer's baptism, and are twenty-one or older
may declare to the church community their request to
take lifelong vows of membership.

Before taking vows, candidates must first settle all their
worldly affairs. They must give away all their property
in obedience to the gospel, so that at the time of taking   *Luke 12:32–34; 18:22–30*
vows they own absolutely nothing. They are free to
do this in whatever way they think right, whether
by donating to the church community or otherwise.
Our concern is not money or goods, but God-fearing   *Heb 12:28–29*
hearts. Membership in any other church or denomi-
nation must be terminated. In addition, they must
fully disclose their personal history, including all

debts and outstanding commitments; any wrong dealings, criminal convictions, or acts punishable by law; and continuing obligations to anyone, including to children or to former or present spouses or partners. To enter membership while willfully hiding such

Acts 5:1–11

matters or keeping back any possessions would be a grave sin of deception.

If the church community discerns that such a request is based on a clear call from God, it may decide to receive the candidate into membership. Membership vows are taken at a celebratory meeting of the church community where the vows are publicly professed.

Our Vows

Luke 14:33; Num 14:24
Acts 4:32–33; Phil 3:7–9
1 Tim 6:11–12

38 The act of taking vows is a sign of giving oneself completely and binding oneself unreservedly to the service of Christ in church community. Through this solemn and public act we pledge to no longer claim anything for ourselves, out of love to Christ. Our example is Mary the mother of Jesus, who said:

Luke 1:38 NRSV

"Here am I, the servant of the Lord; let it be with me according to your word."

Matt 16:25

Jesus told those who wished to follow him: "Whoever would save his life will lose it, and whoever loses his life for my sake will find it." He also taught: "When

Luke 17:10

you have done all that is commanded you, say, 'We are unworthy servants; we have only done what was our duty.'" It is in this sense that we take our vows.

39 Vows of membership are made in the spirit of the traditional monastic vows of poverty, chastity, and obedience:

Poverty: We pledge to give up all property and to live simply, in complete freedom from possessions.

Luke 12:32–34; 2 Cor 9:7–8
Matt 6:25–32

Chastity: We pledge to uphold sexual purity and, if married, to stay faithful in the bond of marriage between one man and one woman for life.

Matt 5:27–32; 1 Cor 6:9–10
Heb 13:4
Matt 19:3–9

Obedience: We pledge to yield ourselves up in obedience to Christ and our brothers and sisters, promising to serve the church community wherever and however we are asked.

1 Pet 1:1–2
John 13:13–17; Eph 5:21

40 Vows of membership are made publicly, to God and before the church community, by answering the following questions:

1. Do you promise to proclaim Jesus in word and deed, for the rest of your life?

    Mark 16:15–20; Luke 12:8–9
    Rom 1:14–17; 15:17–20

2. Are you certain that this way of brotherly and sisterly community, based on a firm faith in God and in Jesus Christ, is the way to which God has called you?

    2 Tim 1:12
    John 15:15–17

3. Are you willing, for the sake of Christ, to put yourself completely at the disposal of the church community to the end of your life – all your faculties, the entire strength of your body and

    Rom 12:1–2

Acts 4:34–37

soul, and all your property, both that which you now possess and that which you may later inherit or earn?

Matt 18:15–17

Luke 17:3–4; Col 3:15–16

4. Will you accept admonition, when justified, and will you yourself admonish others if you sense within our community life something that should be clearer or would more fittingly express the will of God?

Luke 15:7; Acts 3:17–26

1 Pet 4:17; Rev 2—3

2 Cor 7:8–13

5. Because a living church will always be a repenting church, do you affirm and uphold the practice of church discipline, and will you be ready to ask for it yourself if necessary?*

Gal 6:9–10; Heb 10:23–25

6. Are you firmly decided to remain loyal and true, bound with us in the service of love as brothers and sisters in building up church community, outreach to all people, and the proclamation of the gospel?

Upon answering yes, the new member receives the laying on of hands in the prayer that God will fill him or her anew with the Holy Spirit.

Deut 23:21; Acts 5:4

Eccl 5:1–7

41 Because vows of membership are made to God, no human being has the authority to dissolve them. Accordingly, if members leave our fellowship, the church community has no obligation to return any property or to remunerate them for the labor or anything else they may have contributed while they lived within it. To do so would violate the vow to

---

* See Section 76 below.

renounce all possessions. Any who are unsure about *Luke 9:62*
such a commitment should rather stay away, keep what
is theirs, and leave us in peace. *Luke 14:28–33*

While we are accountable to God and our brothers
and sisters for our vows, no one should remain in our
church community who does not do so "with joy and *Acts 2:46–47*
to the delight of his soul."* Members who leave our
fellowship are provided with transitional support. Such
assistance is not a right, but is offered at the discretion
of the church community, as an expression of its
continuing love.

The Responsibility of Membership

42 The church community is made manifest through the
body of all members worldwide under lifelong vows. *1 Cor 12:12–13*
To this body each member and each local community
is accountable. In all it does it must act in deepest *Acts 15:1–35*
reverence for the Holy Spirit and for the mystery of *Eph 3*
Christ's church. The convening of this body is referred
to as a "worldwide membership meeting."

The membership of a local community (referred to as
a "Bruderhof") is only a constituent part of the worldwide body of members. Following the example of the
itinerant early Christians, members must be ready to *Mark 16:15; Acts 16—21*
live at any Bruderhof or any other place, as the needs
of the church community as a whole may require.

---

* "Ten Points: What the Church of God Is and How One Is Led into It,"
church teaching included in the Hutterian baptismal instruction known
as the *Taufbüchlein* (ca. 1528–1600).

As part of this greater whole, each individual Bruderhof forms a distinct household, having a unique name,
character, and expression. Each Bruderhof orders its
own life as an individual fellowship of believers, yet in
connection with its sister communities.

Rom 16:5; Col 4:15
1 Cor 16:15–19

Rom 15:23–33

43 The worldwide body of members bears the final
responsibility before God for the spiritual and
temporal life of the church community: its faith, unity,
mission, work, church order, daily life, deeds of charity,
and the education and health in body and soul of
everyone in the communal household.

Acts 6:1–7

To carry out these responsibilities, the membership
appoints individual members to various tasks of leadership, giving them its trust and authorizing them to
represent it inside and outside the church community.
They are accountable to the body of members in the
fear of God for the tasks entrusted to them.

Acts 11:29–30; 14:23

Exod 18

Heb 13:17

44 In keeping with the biblical teaching of the priest-
hood of all believers, the collective responsibility for
the spiritual life of church community rests on each
member individually, as a matter of conscience. Our
common life belongs to Christ; each member must
ensure that nothing but Christ's love fills and guides us.

1 Pet 2:5–9
Eph 4:11–13

Jas 4:17; Rom 14:22–23

No excuse relieves any member of this responsibility.
If anything is wrong in the church community, every
member without exception has the responsibility
before God to work tirelessly to reestablish the rule of

Heb 3:12–13; 10:24–25

Col 1:28–29

Christ among us. This means persevering in humility, without fear of man, sparing no effort or sacrifice, until the matter is set right. The church community thus depends on the faith of each member.

2 Cor 2:4

Acts 20:26–35; Phil 4:1–3

Eph 4:16

45 There are times when a member estranges himself or herself from the church community, for example by leaving its fellowship or by willfully violating his or her vows. Any member so estranged ceases to be a member in good standing.

Titus 3:10–11

1 Jn 2:19; 3 Jn 1:9–11

Only members in good standing are to be regarded as members in the sense described in these pages; in partic-ular, only they may participate in the life of the church community, remain on the grounds of a Bruderhof, serve in positions of spiritual or temporal responsibility, or represent the church community publicly.

In case of doubt, it is for the body of members, spoken for by its appointed leadership, to declare whether or not a person is a member in good standing. We will go to great lengths to reconcile with any member not in good standing, in the hope that he or she may be restored to full fellowship.

Jude 1:20–23; Jas 5:19–20

A Variety of Gifts

46 In our fellowship, "there are varieties of gifts, but the same Spirit; and there are varieties of service, but the same Lord; and there are varieties of working, but it is the same God who inspires them all in every one. To each is given the manifestation of the Spirit for

1 Cor 12:4–7

the common good." Some members receive the gift to teach, some to counsel and encourage, some to proclaim the gospel, some to praise God through music and art, some to care for the needy, some to contribute in other practical ways. But the greatest gift, offered to each of us, is the ability to love.

Rom 12:3–8

1 Cor 13:13; Gal 5:6

Just as the various parts of the human body work together selflessly, so the members of Christ's body should serve one another. Each Bruderhof, in connection with its sister communities, appoints brothers and sisters to be responsible for the various spiritual and practical aspects of the common life: pastoral leadership; stewardship of money and goods; education of children and youth; work departments such as the farm, workshop, kitchen, and offices; and hospitality. In this, we follow the example of the early church with its elders and overseers, deacons and deaconesses, teachers, and widows.

John 13:1–17; Gal 5:13

1 Tim 3:8–13; 5:1–16

47 Whatever our gifts and responsibilities, we must use them to advance God's glory, never our own. God can work through us only if our personal power – our desire for influence, recognition, and success – is dismantled and put away. This does not happen in a single heroic decision, but piece by piece, through the constant working of grace. If we assert our own power even a little, God's spirit and authority will retreat from our lives to the same degree. But if we are spiritually poor, he can use us as his instruments to build up his church.

John 15:8; 1 Pet 2:12

2 Cor 12:8–9; Jer 9:23–24

Phil 2:12–13; 3:12–14

John 3:27–30

Matt 5:3; 1 Cor 1:18–31

40

Pastoral Leadership

48 The service of pastoral leadership was instituted by
Christ himself when he made the apostle Peter the
shepherd of the first church, asking him, "Do you love   *John 21:15–19*
me?" and commanding him, "Feed my sheep." We
affirm the shepherd's task in this sense as a gift of God   *1 Thess 5:12–13; Heb 13:17*
to the church.

49 Leadership must be based on trust. Such trust has to
be earned; no one can demand it as a right by virtue   *1 Cor 9:1–18*
of office. Pastoral leadership does not depend on fixed
offices, natural talents, or seminary training, but on
God's grace and the working of the Spirit. Not even the   *Eph 4:7–13; Num 11:24–25*
most gifted person has anything to say in the church   *1 Sam 16:14*
community if what he represents is himself.   *2 Cor 3:4–6; 4:5*

A person entrusted with leadership must always let
himself be guided by the Holy Spirit. He must remain   *John 14:26; Zech 4:6*
deeply humble and must honor and respect the body   *Num 12:3*
of members. Under no circumstances may he force   *2 Cor 1:24; 1 Thess 2:7–12*
anything on those around him; he is not placed in this
task to control or dominate, but to serve. When Jesus   *1 Pet 5:3; 2 Tim 2:24–26*
entrusted his church to Peter, he did not give him any
rights over the other disciples. Instead he taught: "The   *Matt 20:25–28 NRSV*
rulers of the Gentiles lord it over them, and their great
ones are tyrants over them. It will not be so among
you; but whoever wishes to be great among you must
be your servant, and whoever wishes to be first among
you must be your slave; just as the Son of Man came
not to be served but to serve, and to give his life a
ransom for many."

50 Because pastoral leadership means service, we call those who carry this responsibility "servants of the Word." According to the New Testament, this task can be given only to a brother who fulfills scriptural requirements as regards his personal conduct and life of faith.

1 Tim 2:11–12; 3:1–7

Titus 1:5–9

Any brother who is baptized and has taken membership vows can be suggested for the service of the Word by any other member, and if the church community agrees, he may be appointed. If he is married, he does this service together with his wife, who shares and is essential to his particular obligation to care for souls. An appointment to the service of the Word is made on a trial basis. If after a time of testing and preparation a brother's service is unanimously recognized as given by God, the appointment will be publicly confirmed through the laying on of hands on him and his wife, conferring the authority of the church.

Acts 14:21—15:2

Acts 18:26; 1 Cor 9:5

2 Cor 12:15

1 Tim 4:14

Each Bruderhof usually has several servants of the Word. They work together as a pastoral team among themselves and with the other brothers and sisters who are responsible for the various spiritual and temporal aspects of the common life.

Acts 14:23; 20:17

51 The task of a servant of the Word is to care for all in the church community in body and soul and to witness to the gospel.

1 Pet 5:1–4; 1 Tim 4:12–16

A servant of the Word's main concern should be pastoral care. He and his wife are called to bear the compassion of Christ toward each person, with the goal

John 21:15–17

that each one can flourish with the fullness of life of the *John 10:10* gospel. They both must seek to be led by the Spirit in offering counsel and guidance in reverence for any soul *Acts 20:28–35; Gal 6:1* who turns to them for advice or to find freedom from sin through confession. *Jas 5:14–16*

A servant of the Word is charged to express that which *1 Cor 2:12–16* is from God and which moves in the hearts of the members. He is authorized to baptize, to serve the *Matt 16:18–19* Lord's Supper, to perform weddings, and to pronounce forgiveness of sins. A servant of the Word must be *Matt 28:18–20* ready at all times to be sent out to proclaim the gospel, *2 Tim 4:1–5* wherever the church community may send him.

Ultimately, carrying out the service of the Word simply involves a sharpening and intensification of the responsibilities laid on every member. This also holds true the *1 Pet 2:9* other way around: every member is called to carry out *Gal 6:2; Phil 1:27–28* the shepherd's task in his or her own family and sphere of life, caring for souls and proclaiming the gospel.

52 Just as a ship needs a helmsman, so the church *Eph 4:11–13* community needs clear leadership. For this reason, the body of members unanimously commissions one brother for the shepherd's task for the church community as a whole, to serve together with his wife for as long as he is able. Known as the elder, he is entrusted to the fullest degree with the care of souls, the spiritual oversight of all communities, the order and authority of the church, and the proclamation of the gospel.

Like every other servant of the Word, the elder must follow the guidance of the Holy Spirit speaking among the members. He must not isolate himself or put his trust in his own abilities. In deep humility and in close cooperation with the body of members and all those it has appointed to various tasks, a clear direction in all matters can be found.

1 Cor 2:1–5; 2 Cor 3:4–6

53 To support the elder in his task, the members may appoint servants of the Word as bishops who care for the communities in a particular geographic region. Bishops are responsible not just to the members of the communities they serve, but to the elder and the world-wide body of members.

Titus 1:5

54 If anyone appointed to a service of leadership falls into serious sin or abuses his position, or if his service is ineffective or harmful, he should lay it down, or he will be relieved of his service by the body of members. In accordance with our vows, each member has a duty to intervene if someone is misusing a position of leadership.

1 Tim 5:20

If there is a question of relieving the elder of his service, this step, in light of its seriousness, can be taken only by the worldwide body of members after meeting day by day for prayerful consideration and in the fear of God, heedful of Scripture's warning never to admit a charge against a church leader except on the evidence of two or three witnesses.

1 Tim 5:19

44

55 In a church united by love, the service of leadership will always point to Christ. Among us we know no difference in rank. We are all brothers and sisters, all members of the one body, each serving the other. Governing this body is its sole head, Jesus Christ.

Col 1:28–29

Matt 23:8–12

Eph 1:22–23

Making Decisions

56 Decisions in the church community should be the expression of a unanimity freely arrived at through common discernment and prayer within the fellowship of believers. Unanimity in decision-making is a fruit of the unity of the body of Christ, to which we seek to belong. It comes from listening together to God's Spirit, who speaks the same message to all who desire to hear him, in practical as well as spiritual questions.

Acts 15:1–35

Acts 4:31–32; Eph 4:1–6

John 16:13

We therefore reject decision-making by democratic or congregational vote. The rule of human opinions, whether of the majority or the minority, is the enemy of the rule of the Holy Spirit, and accordingly the checks and balances of representational government are not of God's kingdom.

1 Cor 1:10–17

57 Unanimity in the Spirit is not conformity. It cannot be manufactured through consensus-building, persuasion, or pressure. In our experience, the dissent of a single voice has at times proved to be prophetic. Members must be able to speak their minds freely, especially in matters of conscience. A false unanimity produced by conformism or fear drives away the spirit of Christ.

Rom 12:3–8; 1 Pet 4:10–11

Rom 14; 1 Cor 8

45

If we are unable to come to agreement, the reason may simply be that the moment is not yet ripe for a decision, or it may be that members feel differently on a particular matter of conscience. In that case, the matter should be left open for the time being. Then the Spirit must lead us to a common conviction that each can embrace naturally and from the heart.

Phil 3:15–16

On the other hand, a lack of unanimity may be caused by something quite concrete that is blocking us from hearing God's will together – for instance, wounded vanity, hidden grudges, selfishness, or arrogance on the part of many or a few. In that case, these hindrances must be recognized and overcome, so that we do not become guilty of disobeying the Spirit out of human pettiness.

Titus 1:10–14

1 Thess 5:19; Eph 4:29–30

58 Local communities are autonomous in directing their day-to-day administration. Nevertheless, they serve in connection with sister communities around the world. We entrust each bishop with oversight for the communities within his assigned region and the elder with general oversight for all communities, exceeded only by the authority of the body of members at a worldwide membership meeting. The elder is the authorized spokesman of the body of members. He will honor local communities' decisions as having great weight, yet he may object to them or even set them aside until the body of members has considered the matter. Each member is free at any time to bring his or her concerns directly to the regional bishop or to the elder.

2 Cor 8

46

No Law but Love

59 There is no law but that of love.* Love is joy in others. *Matt 22:35–40; Rom 13:10*
To preserve this love, Christ teaches us to speak directly *Jas 2:8; Gal 5:14*
to our brother or sister whenever there is anything *Matt 18:15–20*
between us. We are to make peace with our brother or *Eph 4:25–27*
sister before the sun goes down; Christ even warns us
to stay away from common prayer until we have done
so: "If you are offering your gift at the altar, and there *Matt 5:23–24*
remember that your brother has something against
you, leave your gift there before the altar and go; first
be reconciled to your brother, and then come and offer
your gift."

It is therefore out of the question for someone in our *Jas 4:11–12*
community to hold something against a brother or
sister or to talk behind his or her back. Relationships
within and to the church community are spiritual
bonds based on trust and on the readiness to forgive *Luke 17:3–4; 2 Cor 6:11–13*
again and again. *Gen 42–50*

60 Like the early Christians and those faithful to their
example through the ages, we insist on the need for *1 Thess 5:14; Col 3:16*
mutual fraternal admonition. Misunderstandings,
conflicts, and honest differences of opinion are bound *Acts 15:36–41; Gal 2:1–14*
to arise, and this does not surprise or disturb us. But
whenever there is tension between brothers and
sisters, we must use the way of direct address taught by
Christ. We owe this service to anyone in the church

---

* House rule of the first Bruderhof community in Sannerz, Germany
(1925).

community whose real or imagined weaknesses cause a negative reaction in us. A frank word spoken and received in love and humility serves only to deepen friendship and renew trust. If our concern turns out to be unjustified, so much the better.

If two people are unable to come to peace on their own, it is necessary to take the additional steps that Jesus sets forth in Matthew 18: first to draw in one or two others to help; and then, as a last resort, to lay the situation before the church to be resolved by its *Matt 18:17–18* authority. According to Christ's teaching, anyone who refuses at that point to listen even to the assembled church should leave and go his or her own way.

Rom 16:17–20; 1 Cor 1:10–13 Likewise, if there is division in the church community or abuse of authority by its leadership, the matter will *1 Tim 5:19–20* if necessary be brought before the worldwide body of members for final resolution, in the prayer that the Spirit may lead to clarity, repentance, and renewed love. All conflicts within the church community can and must be settled in this way. In accordance with *Matt 5:25–26; 1 Cor 6:1–8* Scripture, they may never be taken to any adjudicator outside the church community, certainly not to a court of law.*

---

* A criminal act by anyone living on a Bruderhof is not an internal church matter and will be subject to legitimate state authority.

5

CHURCH ACTIONS

61 The kingdom of God is not a concept, but a living
reality that surpasses human understanding. To explain
this mystery, Jesus used parables – simple stories from
everyday life. In the same way, he instituted certain
simple actions for his church as signs of the power of
his kingdom: the washing with water in baptism; the
communal breaking of bread and drinking of wine at
the Lord's Supper; the laying on of hands to pronounce
forgiveness or pray for healing; the granting of church
discipline and reacceptance; and the joining of husband
and wife in marriage. Since early Christian times, these
actions have been known as sacraments: sacred symbols
that give visible form to the hidden reality of Christ in
our midst.

Is 55:6–11; Rom 11:33–36

Eph 3:17–21

Matt 13

These symbolic actions are nothing miraculous in
themselves. Instead, they are signs of the prayer of the
united church interceding for God to act, illustrating
the working of Christ. They are seals of the authority

Acts 8:17–21

Jas 5:13–16

Matt 16:19; 18:18–20
1 Cor 11:27–32
Heb 10:19–25; 12:28–29

he gave to the church by entrusting it with the keys of the kingdom. We may approach them only with the utmost reverence.

Baptism

Matt 28:19–20 NRSV

62 Baptism is a command of Christ: "Go therefore and make disciples of all nations, baptizing them in the name of the Father and of the Son and of the Holy Spirit, and teaching them to obey everything that I have commanded you."

Mark 16:15–16; Acts 2:38–41
Matt 3:7–8; Acts 26:19–20
Rom 1:16

In obedience to this commission, the church community offers baptism to every person who believes in the gospel of Jesus Christ and whose repentance comes from the heart, bearing fruit in deeds. In order to receive believer's baptism as instituted by Christ for the forgiveness of sins, a person must have reached the age of accountability.

Matt 3:1–11
Luke 24:49
Acts 10:44–48

Anyone who has been commissioned by the church community may baptize people as John the Baptist did, "with water." Then he will lay his hands on the newly baptized and pray that Jesus will fill them with "power from on high" – with the Holy Spirit.

Matt 28:19

Rom 6:1–14; Gal 2:20

63 The form of baptism was set by Christ himself: washing with water in the name of the Father, the Son, and the Holy Spirit. Immersion in water symbolizes dying, being reborn, and rising with Christ to a new life of righteousness, through Christ's victory on the cross.

50

The pouring over of water symbolizes the washing away of sins and the outpouring of the Spirit.

Matt 3:11; Acts 19:1–7; 22:16

The method of baptism that may be used – whether immersion or pouring over – is unimportant. What matters is the intervention of God to fully cleanse, forgive, and heal the one baptized.

John 4:23–24

John 1:12–13; 13:2–10

64 Baptism is the declaration of a good conscience with God. Through it the church witnesses to and seals salvation in the name of Christ. "For by grace you have been saved through faith; and this is not your own doing, it is the gift of God." At Pentecost, when many in the crowd were "cut to the heart" after realizing their guilt for the death of Christ, three thousand were baptized in one day. Such repentance and the conversion that follows it are the only sure foundations for baptism.

1 Pet 3:21

Acts 4:12

Eph 2:8

Acts 2:37–41

John 3:1–8

True repentance is a gift of God. It is recognizable by a remorseful and contrite heart, a desire to confess one's sins, and a changed life that shows fruits of a new spirit. One who truly repents will be determined never to sin willfully anymore, but rather to die than disobey God.

Pss 32; 51

Matt 3:6; Acts 19:17–20

2 Tim 2:19; Titus 2:11–14

Heb 12:1–17; 1 Jn 3:6

1 Pet 3:13–4:6

65 Baptism is a confession of faith – faith in Jesus of Nazareth, the son of Mary and son of God, who was born in poverty, died on the cross, rose from the dead, and will one day return to establish his kingdom fully on earth. Before a baptism is carried out in our church community, the candidate proclaims his or her faith in

Acts 22:16; 1 Tim 6:12–16

Phil 2:5–11; 1 Tim 3:16

1 Cor 15:1–8 Jesus and affirms all the points of the Christian faith as stated in the Apostles' and Nicene Creeds.

Luke 9:23–25, 62 **66** Baptism is a pledge to follow Jesus, come what may, obeying him in everything. The early Christians taught *2 Tim 2:3–10; 2 Cor 10:3–5* that just as a recruit becomes a soldier through taking *Eph 6:10–20* an oath of allegiance, so baptism enlists us as soldiers for Christ, sworn to his service even at the cost of our lives.*

67 Baptism is therefore also incorporation into the body *1 Cor 12:12–13 NRSV* of Christ, "for in the one Spirit we were all baptized *Gal 3:26–28* into one body." Through baptism we become fellow members with all believers through the ages, sharing *Eph 4:4–6* in "one body and one Spirit...one Lord, one faith, one baptism, one God and Father of us all, who is above all and through all and in all." Anyone who belongs to Christ will join with others who also belong to him: *Matt 12:30* "He who does not gather with me scatters."

The Lord's Supper

Luke 22:14–19 **68** On the last evening before his death, Christ asked his disciples to remember him with a simple meal of bread and wine. We celebrate the Lord's Supper in obedience to him, seeking to keep to simplicity and reverence.

69 The Lord's Supper is first of all a meal of remembrance: *1 Cor 11:24* "Do this in remembrance of me." Through sharing

---

* *First Letter of Clement,* 37.1–4 (ca. AD 80–100); Ignatius of Antioch, *Letter to Polycarp,* 6.2 (ca. AD 98–117).

it, we are reminded of Christ's life, his death, his resurrection, and his promise to come again.

70 The Lord's Supper is a meal of communion with Christ, for while eating it with his disciples, Jesus said, "This is my body....This is my blood." He also said: *Matt 26:26–28; 1 Cor 10:16* "He who eats my flesh and drinks my blood abides in *John 6:56* me, and I in him." By partaking of the bread and wine, we renew our covenant of baptism, giving ourselves to Jesus in full surrender and declaring our readiness to suffer and die for him. We believe that he himself will *John 12:24–25; Col 1:24* be present among us with his power to heal the sick, *John 14:11–14* forgive sins, and drive out evil.

71 The Lord's Supper is a meal of unity. Together we *1 Cor 10:17; 11:33–34* declare ourselves united under God's judgment and mercy.

In this meal, the church is set apart from every other body and association. The early church taught that only those who are baptized, tested in daily life, and united in fellowship with the church community should take part.* Out of the same reverence, we also celebrate *1 Cor 10:16–22; 11:27–32* the Lord's Supper only with those who have received believer's baptism, who affirm the same confession of faith, and with whom there is peace and unity. If before this meal we become aware of anything that stands between us and God or between us and brothers and

---

* *Didache,* 9.5, 14.1–3 (ca. AD 60–110); Justin Martyr, *First Apology,* chapter 66 (ca. AD 151–155).

Matt 5:23–24 sisters, we must first make peace so that we can come to Christ's table with free hearts.

According to an early Christian tradition, bread and wine are themselves a symbol of unity.* To make bread, grains from different fields are harvested and baked into a single loaf; to make wine, grapes from different vineyards are collected and pressed to yield a single vintage. In the same way, the church is gathered from many lands and nations to be made one in Christ.

1 Cor 11:23–26 **72** The Lord's Supper is a meal of thanksgiving, a celebration of Christ's victory over sin and death. Through it we proclaim his death until he comes again. This feast is a foretaste of his return – the great wedding banquet *Rev 19:6–9* foretold in Scripture, when he will come as bridegroom to unite with his bride, the church.

The Laying on of Hands

Matt 16:19 **73** Christ gives the church the authority to act on his behalf. The laying on of hands is a symbol of this *Gen 48:14* authority, used from earliest times by the people of God to ask him to give his blessing, to set a person *Num 11:16–25; 27:15–23* apart for himself in a special way, or to bestow the power of his Spirit.

Jesus and his apostles used this sign – sometimes *Jas 5:13–20* together with anointing – to forgive sins, heal the *Luke 4:40; 8:40–56* sick, raise the dead, drive out demons, give blessings, *Acts 8:14–17; 13:1–3* commission messengers of the gospel, and pray for the

---

* *Didache*, 9.4 (ca. AD 60–110).

Spirit to fill the believers. As members of Christ's body, we are charged to do the same. Among us, this church action usually takes place in a worship meeting when a servant of the Word places his hands on the head of the person concerned and says a prayer of intercession.

Mark 16:15–18

The laying on of hands is also used to dedicate a newborn child. We do this after the example of Jesus, who laid his hands on little children and prayed for them. When parents present their baby to the gathered community, they acknowledge that the child belongs to God. In a special prayer, the child receives a blessing and the parents are commissioned to raise the little one in God's stead.

Luke 2:22–38

Matt 19:13–15

Eph 6:1–4; Deut 6:7
Ps 78:4–8

Church Discipline and Forgiveness

74 Christ entrusted the church with the gift of church discipline, commissioning it to confront and overcome sin and to declare forgiveness in his name to the repentant: "I will give you the keys of the kingdom of heaven, and whatever you bind on earth shall be bound in heaven, and whatever you loose on earth shall be loosed in heaven." "If you forgive the sins of any, they are forgiven; if you retain the sins of any, they are retained."

Matt 18:15–20
1 Cor 5:1–13; Lev 19:17
Luke 17:1–4
Matt 16:19

John 20:23

To be a disciple involves discipline – training and correction – through Christ and his church: "Those whom I love, I reprove and discipline." We continue to need this gift throughout our lives. None of us is without sin, and there is no shame in admitting this.

John 15:1–4; Deut 8:5–6
Rev 3:19 ESV
Prov 3:11–12; Job 5:17
1 Jn 1:8–10

Luke 24:47; Acts 26:18
Luke 15; Mark 2:17
Luke 7:36–50; 1 Pet 4:8
Luke 15:7, 10
Mic 7:18–20

That is why Christ gave the church the power to forgive all sins in his name. Forgiveness is at the heart of his gospel, for those who are forgiven much, love much. Christ teaches: "There will be more joy in heaven over one sinner who repents than over ninety-nine righteous persons who need no repentance."

Jas 5:16
Ps 51; 2 Sam 12:13

Ps 34:18; Is 57:15
2 Cor 7:8–11

75 The New Testament instructs us to "confess your sins to one another." Such confession is a fruit of repentance and must be entirely voluntary. It is necessary before baptism, and just as important afterward. If we do this with a contrite heart, in the determination not to sin again, the power of sin is broken.*

1 Cor 6:9–11; Gal 5:19–21
Rev 21:8; 1 Cor 5:6–8
Eph 5:8–17, 27
1 Pet 1:13–16; Lev 20:26
John 15:1–6
1 Cor 5:5; 2 Jn 1:7–11
Mark 9:42–50; Matt 25:1–13

Luke 13:22–30

2 Cor 2:5–11

76 As the New Testament teaches, certain sinful actions are particularly serious. They affect not only the person responsible but also the whole church, harming its life and witness as the consecrated body of Christ. Those who commit such sins depart from the church's peace and unity; in fact, Scripture warns that they place themselves outside the kingdom of God. To be restored to fellowship, such brothers and sisters need to give an account to the church for their actions and then reenter it through the same door by which they entered at baptism – that is, through repentance, confession, and forgiveness. This is possible through the gift of church discipline.

---

* Dietrich Bonhoeffer, "Confession and the Lord's Supper," in *Life Together* (*Gemeinsames Leben,* 1939; published in English 1954).

Church discipline is available to an adult baptized believer who wishes to undertake a time of repentance in order to be reconciled to God and the church. It is a time of silent reflection when the person concerned steps back from full participation in the common life. Through silence, one gains freedom from everyday concerns so that the heart can become quiet. It is a chance to cleanse one's conscience of all that burdens it and to stand before God. Throughout such a time, the church community shows its redoubled love to those in discipline, caring for their practical needs with special consideration and keeping them constantly in its prayers. We each stand with them in our need of God's judgment and forgiveness.

Pss 62:1–2; 131

Joel 2:12–13; Ezek 36:25–27

Luke 15:22–24; Gal 6:9–10

Luke 18:9–14; 1 Pet 5:5–7

Understood rightly, church discipline is a grace, a sign of God's mercy, and an act of hope. In our church community, the gift of discipline is granted only to those who desire and request it. It is not a punishment and has nothing in common with shunning, expulsion, or any kind of coercion; to abuse it for any such purpose is a sin. Rather, members who undertake a time of discipline remain our brothers and sisters and continue to be members in good standing.* In seeking repentance, they do a service for Christ and his kingdom.

Heb 12:3–13

2 Thess 3:15

Rev 2—3

---

* By contrast, an unrepentant person who rejects the help of the church community while persisting in sin cannot be granted church discipline. In such a case, according to Christ's instructions in Matthew 18, the church community may ultimately need to separate ways from the one concerned; for a member, this results in loss of membership in good standing (see Section 45). Such separation is not a form of church discipline, but merely an acknowledgment by the church community that continued fellowship is impossible. The church community will continue to pray for the person in the constant hope for reconciliation.

When a person in discipline has gained the assurance of a cleansed heart and God's peace, he or she may ask to be reaccepted into the fellowship of the church community. The church then declares the forgiveness of sins, receiving the person back with joy and unreserved love.

2 Cor 2:5–11

Eph 4:30–32; Rom 15:5–7

Marriage

77 Christ declared marriage to be the lifelong union of one man and one woman joined together by God, holy and instituted by him from the beginning: "From the beginning of creation, 'God made them male and female.' 'For this reason a man shall leave his father and mother and be joined to his wife, and the two shall become one flesh.' So they are no longer two, but one flesh. Therefore what God has joined together, let no one separate."

Mark 10:6–9 NRSV

Gen 1:27; 5:2

Gen 2:24

Jesus had great joy in marriage and performed his first miracle at a wedding by changing water to wine. We too rejoice whenever a man and a woman are led by God to love each other and vow to be faithful to each other for life. In the church community, marriage vows are made publicly before the gathered members as witnesses, and the marriage is then confirmed by the church through the laying on of hands.

John 2:1–11

78 As a creation of God, marriage is not a human invention. It is a sacrament that precedes and transcends the authority of the state. When a man and a woman

Matt 19:6

58

become one flesh in marriage, their union has a deep
connection with God. He made man and woman
for each other, each in his image and likeness, and *1 Cor 11:11–12; Gen 1:26–27*
yet each incomplete without the other. He intended *Gen 2:18–24*
their union – a relationship unlike any other – for the
bearing and rearing of children. In a true marriage, *Gen 1:28; 9:1*
husband and wife will have an attitude of welcome *Mark 9:37; Ps 127:3–5*
toward the conception and birth of new life, even if this
seems unlikely or impossible in their individual case.

Christ honors the mystery of marriage so highly that he *Matt 5:27–32*
demands a life of chastity. Sex is a gift from God, but if *Song 2:16; 1 Cor 7:3–7*
it is isolated from him and his will, it defiles the soul;
apart from marriage, it is sin. The Bible clearly requires *Heb 13:4; 1 Thess 4:3–8*
abstinence before marriage and outside of it. In fact, *Prov 5:1–20*
Jesus warns us that even a lustful glance is adultery *Matt 5:28*
of the heart.

79 Since marriage is the lifelong union between one *Matt 19:3–9*
man and one woman according to God's creative will,
and since God intended sexual love to be shared only *1 Cor 6:12–20*
between a husband and a wife, the church community
can never recognize a homosexual relationship as a *Rom 1:21–32; 1 Cor 6:9–11*
marriage, regardless of whether it is termed as such
by law or society.

We are called to represent God's love toward every *John 3:16–17*
person, including those who experience same-sex
attractions. We condemn no one. Yet Christ declares: *John 8:3–11*
"If any want to become my followers, let them deny *Luke 9:23 NRSV*
themselves and take up their cross daily and follow me."

Matt 7:13–14

Matt 11:28–30

Titus 2:11–14

He calls every disciple to keep to this narrow way. The church community welcomes into its midst all who are willing to accept Christ's call and to forsake everything for him.

80 With regard to divorce and remarriage, Christ says:

Mark 10:2–12

Matt 5:32; 19:9; Luke 16:18

"Whoever divorces his wife and marries another, commits adultery against her; and if she divorces her husband and marries another, she commits adultery."

Matt 28:20

The church community must uphold Jesus' teaching, which is the only stand consistent with real truthfulness and love. Even if separation should occur in isolated cases, no member of the church community

Rom 7:1–3; 1 Cor 7:10–11

may divorce his or her spouse. Further, no divorced member may remarry if a former spouse is still living.

81 The callings of man and woman in marriage are

Gal 3:28

Eph 5:22–33

different, yet equal in worth. According to the New Testament, the husband is to be the head of the family, and the wife his helper. He must never dominate her,

Col 3:19

but should cherish and serve her in humility. At a wedding in our communities, the bridegroom promises to always honor and respect his bride, and is reminded

1 Pet 3:7

of the apostle Peter's warning that if he neglects this, God may refuse his prayers. Likewise, a wife should support her husband in what is good. Above all, both

1 Jn 4:7–21

spouses alike are charged with leading each other closer to Christ.

Marriage is a great good, but not the greatest. For a believer, Christ must always come before everything, including the desire to marry (if single) or the commitment to one's spouse (if married). In our communities, members can enter into marriage only with the blessing of the church community. Each of our marriages must be founded on a shared faith in Christ and dedicated to his service. At a wedding, bride and bridegroom promise never to follow each other in what is wrong, but to place obedience to Christ and his church above their bond to each other. This promise protects the foundation on which Christian marriage is built.

Matt 19:10–12

1 Cor 7:39; 2 Cor 6:14–18

Eph 5:21

Luke 14:26

82 The New Testament speaks of the union of bride and bridegroom as a sacred mystery, a symbol of Christ's love for the church. Jesus himself compared the kingdom of God to a wedding feast. Here we gain a glimpse of the deepest meaning of marriage: as a sign pointing to the coming of Christ's perfect reign of love.

Eph 5:31–32

Hos 2:14–23

Matt 22:1–14; 25:1–13

Rev 19:6–7

6

LIFE IN COMMUNITY

83 The whole of life in church community must be a
sacrament, a living symbol that illustrates God's calling
for humankind. We do not want to wait for peace
and justice until the day of Christ's return. We wish to
demonstrate a shared life of work and worship in which
the harmony of his coming kingdom can be seen and
touched today, in our daily lives.

Eph 3:10–11

Matt 6:33; 2 Cor 5:17–21

1 Pet 2:9–12

2 Pet 3:11–15; Exod 34:10

Outwardly, our communal life will take a variety
of forms, as the Spirit leads. Language, culture, and
customs will differ with time and place. Some of our
communities are rural, and others urban; some are
made up of just a handful of members, while others
number several hundred. Individual members may live
away from our communities for months or years for the
sake of spreading the gospel or undertaking some other
assigned task. Yet pervading all these differences of
circumstance will be the essential unity: our common

From the Sermon on the Mount

Beware of practicing your piety before men in order to be seen by them; for then you will have no reward from your Father who is in heaven.

And in praying do not heap up empty phrases as the Gentiles do; for they think that they will be heard for their many words. Do not be like them, for your Father knows what you need before you ask him. Pray then like this:

> *Our Father who art in heaven,*
> *Hallowed be thy name.*
> *Thy kingdom come.*
> *Thy will be done,*
> *On earth as it is in heaven.*
> *Give us this day our daily bread;*
> *And forgive us our debts,*
> *As we also have forgiven our debtors;*
> *And lead us not into temptation,*
> *But deliver us from evil.*

For if you forgive men their trespasses, your heavenly Father also will forgive you; but if you do not forgive men their trespasses, neither will your Father forgive your trespasses.

Matthew 6:1, 7–15

faith in one baptism, one calling, one profession of *Eph 4:1–6; Gal 3:26–28*
vows, and one Spirit of love who guides us in all things.

Prayer

84 Christ taught us how to pray in the Lord's Prayer, and *Matt 6:9–15*
promised: "Whatever you ask for in prayer, believe that *Mark 11:24 NRSV*
you have received it, and it will be yours." We are to
pray without ceasing. Prayer is the lifeblood of church *1 Thess 5:17*
community, both in the personal life of each member *2 Cor 1:11; Phil 1:19*
and in daily communal gatherings. *Acts 2:42; Eph 6:18*

When we pray together we must approach God
humbly. Spoken prayers are simple. We have no *Matt 6:5–8*
liturgies, no consecrated buildings, but want to worship
"in spirit and truth." We often meet outdoors where the *John 4:21–24*
beauty of nature lifts our hearts and reminds us of the *Ps 121:1–2*
greatness of our Creator.

85 Prayer can take many forms. Silent prayer is an essential *Rom 8:26–27; Ps 46:10*
part of our common life. We also recognize the
importance of voluntary fasting (by adults) as a form *Matt 4:2; 6:16–18*
of intensified prayer. In addition, singing and music can *Acts 13:2–3; Joel 2:12–13*
be a form of prayer. Many of the songs we sing might *Ps 98; Col 3:16*
not appear to be religious at all – songs about nature
or love may best express what moves our hearts and so
bring honor to God, the maker of all things.

Community of Goods

86 Community of goods and a common purse are
the practical expressions of the vocation of church *Acts 2; 4*

community. None of us receives a paycheck, stipend, or allowance from the church community. Once someone has become a member, all of his or her earnings and inheritances are given to the church community, and each receives necessities such as food, clothing, and housing. Each of us is accountable to the church community for money we spend. In our homes and daily lives, we seek to live frugally and give generously, to avoid excess, and to remain unfettered by materialism. In these practical ways we wish to witness that under the stewardship of the church, everything we have is available to anybody in need. This applies especially within our church community: no Bruderhof is to be richer or poorer than another.

1 Tim 6:6–10; Heb 13:5–6
Luke 6:38; Prov 11:24–26
Matt 13:22–23; Luke 12:13–21

Acts 4:34–35
2 Cor 8:13–15

87 Distinct legal entities with appropriate civil-law governance may be established to further the purposes of church community – for example, by holding title to property or operating businesses. Should any such entity ever be dissolved, however, no member would receive anything at all; any assets left would belong to the cause of Christ in church community and to the poor. The statutes of all legal bodies associated with our communities anywhere in the world reflect this understanding.

88 Each Bruderhof appoints a steward to oversee its temporal affairs and to make careful provision for the welfare of every person living within it. Stewards work

Acts 6:1–7

in close collaboration with pastoral leadership. In
this, the steward is accountable to God and to the
body of members.

Common Work

89 Work must be indivisible from prayer, prayer   *Col 3:17, 23–24; Jas 2:26*
indivisible from work. Our work is thus a form of
worship, since our faith and daily life are inseparable,   *Is 58:1–10*
forming a single whole. Even the most mundane task,   *Matt 25:31–46*
if done as for Christ in a spirit of love and dedication,
can be consecrated to God as an act of prayer. To pray
in words but not in deeds is hypocrisy.   *Amos 5:21–24*

Work is a command of God and has intrinsic worth.   *Gen 2:5; 2 Thess 3:6–13*
He gave the earth to humankind to enjoy, cultivate,   *Gen 1:26–28; 2:15*
and care for in reverence as good stewards in his stead.
Therefore, we honor work on the land. We honor
physical work – the exertion of muscle and hand –   *Acts 20:34–35; Eph 4:28*
and the craftsman's creativity and precision. We honor   *Exod 31:3–5*
the activity of the mind and soul too: the inspired work
of the artist, the scholar's exploration of nature and   *Luke 1:1–4*
history, the enterprise of the inventor, the skill of the   *Titus 3:13–14*
professional. Whatever form our work takes, we are
called to do it to the best of our ability in service to
the kingdom of God.

Work within the church community is not primarily
an economic activity valued on the basis of profit or
productivity. No kind of work brings either privilege
or stigma: work in the community laundry is valued as   *1 Cor 12:12–31*

Jas 2:1–9

highly as the work of an expert technician or doctor. We are all brothers and sisters, none higher and none lower. Thus there can be no place in our common life for contractual obligations or relationships based on control, as between a master and servant. We are called to give witness to a different social and economic order based on faith, love, and mutual trust.

Phlm 1:14–16

Matt 20:20–28

90 Because our work is integral to our calling, we cannot accept payment for it from the church community or from one another. Care in the form of food, housing, medical care, and other personal subsistence expenses is received not as a right or in proportion to services rendered, but according to need. Consistent with members' vow of poverty and the faith and practice of our common life, all members, novices, and guests and their dependents who participate in the church community do so on a voluntary basis without expectation of wages, salary, vacation, or compensation of any kind.

Acts 4:34–35

To work in the service of love is our joy. We contribute our talents and energies in whatever ways we are able until the end of our lives. Our vocation is not a trade or profession, but rather the common life itself; none of us has a career. We agree to work wherever we are needed, regardless of our preferences or prior training and experience, ready to change at any time from one task to another.

Luke 19:11–27; 1 Pet 4:10–11

91 Each Bruderhof appoints work distributors to
coordinate the common work. They must attend to
the welfare of all who work and ensure that those
unable to work are cared for.

92 Income from the church community businesses is used
to fulfill our mission: spreading the gospel, building up
and sustaining community life, carrying on educational
work, offering hospitality to visitors, and giving aid to
the needy.

Of necessity, these businesses engage with an economic
system whose values can be at variance with those that   *Luke 16:1–13*
guide our life within the church community. All the
more, every enterprise of the church community must
reflect and yield to our mission and witness, even at the
expense of efficiency or profitability:

Solidarity: Christ's Golden Rule – to do to others as   *Matt 7:12*
we would have done to ourselves – requires solidarity
with all people and respect for their dignity as fellow   *Is 10:1–4*
human beings made in the image of God. To treat
others merely as the means to an economic end is a sin.   *Jas 5:1–6*

Ethical practice: Scripture requires that we act honestly,   *2 Cor 8:16–21; 1 Pet 2:12–17*
respecting the law of the land and having regard for   *Prov 11:1*
the rights and needs of others. The way we conduct   *Deut 5:19–20*
business ought to be a testimony to this.

Workmanship: We strive to work industriously and to   *Prov 6:6–11*
maintain a high quality of workmanship in all we do,   *Exod 35:4—36:7*
as an expression of the love we put into our work.

69

Stewardship of creation: Nature is a work of God that reveals his love and glory; he entrusted it to our care. Reverence for his creation ought to guide us in relation to our use of the earth and its resources.

Ps 19:1–6; Rom 1:20
Ps 8:3–9

We recognize that any income earned by church community businesses is ultimately not our own achievement, but a provision from God to be used for his service.

Deut 8:17–18

Mutual Care

93 Our life together gives us opportunities to show love to one another at every stage of life, from welcoming a newborn baby to attending older brothers and sisters in their last years. Deeds of love are not routine but personal – a matter of following Christ's command to "wash one another's feet." We want to "bear one another's burdens, and so fulfill the law of Christ."

1 Jn 3:16–17
John 13:1–17
Gal 6:2

In doing this, we seek to remember especially those with burdens to carry: widows and widowers, orphans, the disabled and sick, those with mental and emotional ailments, and those who are lonely. Then Jesus' promise will come true: that everyone who has left family and home for his sake will receive back "a hundredfold... houses and brothers and sisters and mothers and children and lands."

Jas 1:27; 1 Tim 5:1–16
Phil 2:25–30
Mark 10:28–31

94 We are grateful for the God-given help of medical science to preserve life and alleviate suffering. We seek to ensure that a high standard of medical care is provided to all brothers, sisters, and children in the church community. Many of our Bruderhofs have doctors and dentists who provide professional care whenever this is appropriate, or support patients who require attention in a hospital.

At the same time, we acknowledge the limits of medicine, particularly at the end of life, recognizing that ultimately our lifespan is determined by God. If a brother or sister decides to decline aggressive medical intervention, for example when facing a terminal illness, that decision is respected. All the more, such a person is surrounded by the prayers, care, and support of brothers and sisters.

Matt 6:27

Job 1:20–21; Deut 32:39

95 Upon a death in our communities, brothers and sisters keep a constant watch around the one who has died during the time before burial, while as many as possible come to take leave. Then the church community gathers to do the last service of love: carrying the body to one of our burial grounds and laying it to rest in the earth until the day of resurrection.

1 Cor 15:51–57

Children and the Family

96 Jesus said, "Let the children come to me, and do not hinder them; for to such belongs the kingdom of heaven." Children belong at the heart of the church community, for they remind us what it means to trust and to be free of heart. We welcome every child, just as Jesus welcomed each one. In all children, and especially

Matt 19:14

Matt 21:16
1 Pet 2:1–3

Matt 18:1–6; Is 11:6

Luke 1:39–45; Ps 139:13–14
Eccl 11:5; Matt 18:10
in the unborn, we recognize the link between human life and eternity.

Gen 1:27–28; 2:21–25
97 The family of father, mother, and children is a creation of God and must be held sacred. Parents have the God-given task of raising their children in his stead. *Eph 6:1–4; Col 3:20–21* Reverence for this relationship between parent and child is the essence of true family life. Such families form the basic unit of church community.

Our communities also include single-parent families. Single parents receive support from fellow members to ensure that their children grow up with both men and women as mentors and role models.

Each family in the church community is provided with its own living quarters in which to make its home in an atmosphere of security and peace. It is important to us to make good use of time at home with our children, including daily meals around the family table, and to avoid work-related distractions and other interruptions.

98 Unmarried men and women form an integral part of our common life. Single people whose families live elsewhere are welcomed into one of the families in their community for meals, weekends, and holidays such as Christmas.

We have reverence for the task of those members who remain single, whether by choice or by circumstance. *1 Cor 7:25–40* They have a noble calling in the service of love, since

they in a special way can give themselves selflessly for
others. In their life of chastity, they give visible witness
to Jesus' call to purity and singleness of heart, testifying
to the fulfillment that comes from leaving all for him.

1 Tim 5:9–10

Matt 19:10–11

Mark 10:28–30

99 Jesus loved his mother and siblings, yet declared in
strong terms that obedience to the gospel must come
before family ties: "While Jesus was still talking to the
crowd, his mother and brothers stood outside, wanting
to speak to him. Someone told him, 'Your mother and
brothers are standing outside, wanting to speak to you.'
He replied to him, 'Who is my mother, and who are my
brothers?' Pointing to his disciples, he said, 'Here are
my mother and my brothers. For whoever does the
will of my Father in heaven is my brother and sister
and mother.'"

John 19:25–27

Luke 14:26; Matt 10:35–37

Matt 12:46–50 NIV

Placing loyalty to Jesus above all else can be difficult,
but his words cannot be ignored. Family relationships
within or beyond the community must not draw us
away from following him.

Luke 9:59–62

Education

100 Church community is a school for young and old in
the discipleship of Christ. True education is a matter of
awakening the soul, of quickening the inner life so that
the whole person is attuned to Christ and his cause.
All members must learn to do concentrated work with
mind and spirit to the full extent of their capabilities.
If we love Christ, we will take an interest in the work of

Titus 2:1–8

Acts 7:22

Acts 14:15–17; Rom 1:18–20
Acts 17:16–31; Dan 1:3–4, 17

God throughout history and will have concern for the social, political, and cultural movements of our time.

101 It is in this context that the education of children and young people takes place. Children should not be molded to conform to the wishes or ambitions of their parents or anyone else. Every child is a thought of God. Education means nurturing the innate divine spark within each child and helping him or her to become the person God intends.

Jer 1:4–5

Deut 5:16; Col 3:20

The Ten Commandments and the New Testament state with good reason, "Honor your father and your mother…that it may go well with you." Children's emotional and spiritual well-being begins in their relationship to their parents; it is parents, not any school or community, who have the primary authority and responsibility for educating their children. Obedience and respect for parents and other adults is the basis of a strong character.

Eph 6:1–4

Prov 6:20–24

Permissiveness and indulgence must be avoided in the education of children, but so too must moralism and legalism. Parents and teachers must be mentors to children as they guide them on their path to adulthood. Anyone who seeks to coerce or assert power over the soul of a child commits a grave sin. Corporal punishment in any form is prohibited.

Mark 7:1–13
Col 2:20–23; 3:21

Matt 18:5–7

102 Where possible, our communities run their own nurseries and schools. Bruderhof schools seek to provide each child with a happy and constructive childhood and to educate the whole child; this includes rigorous academic instruction; craftsmanship and practical skills; singing and the arts; unstructured play and sportsmanship; and the experience of nature. Beyond this, history and literature are studied in a way that traces connections across centuries and cultures.

Our schools emphasize respect, self-discipline, and a strong work ethic. But what matters most is that children develop their capacity to love by caring for and serving others.

1 Tim 4:7–8

2 Pet 1:5–9

103 Adolescence and young adulthood, like childhood, have their own God-given qualities. A church community, just like every other human society, needs the disruptive exuberance of youth and should welcome it, otherwise it cannot remain flexible and alive. We should never force young people to act as if they were grown adults, but should help them to focus their enthusiasm constructively. We must enable them to arrive at their own convictions and, so long as they remain sincere and respectful, to bring their thoughts to expression, even if the result is awkward or unusual.

1 Jn 2:12–14; Eccl 11:9; 12:1

1 Tim 4:12; Jer 1:6–7

After secondary school, many of our young people pursue some form of training at the university level or in a trade (although the church community is under no obligation to provide them with such training). Others find opportunities to volunteer, or learn practical skills in the workplace.

When young people who have grown up within our communities choose other paths in life, the church community will provide support on a case-by-case basis as they establish themselves on their own. We welcome continuing relationships with such young people, provided there is mutual respect. Whether they stay or go, our prayer is that they find God's will in a life of service to others.

Phil 1:9–11

The Individual in Community

104 Just as in a prism we can see the different colors of the spectrum, so in a fellowship of brothers and sisters we will find diverse reflections of God's image. We rejoice in each of these, and reject all attempts to make people uniform. Since all are of equal worth, all must be free to be themselves. The more originality there is among us, the more vibrant our fellowship will be.

1 Cor 12

Rom 15:7

At the same time, we must distinguish between healthy self-determination – being true to one's conscience – and the self-centered individualism that sees everything from its own perspective and seeks its own advantage. While the former is vital in a living community, the latter will destroy it.

Phil 2:1–5

105 Jesus called his disciples "friends" and openly shared his heart with them. In the same way, we should be friends to one another, appreciating each other just as we are with brotherly and sisterly affection.

John 15:14–15

Rom 12:10

76

Each of us has certain natural gifts that make us
unique. But in themselves these are neither a help nor
Phil 3:3–11
a hindrance in serving Christ. We must be liberated
from the whole idea of measuring our own worth, so
that we are neither conceited about our achievements
Eph 2:8–10
nor plagued by feelings of inferiority for our deficits.
Matt 25:14–30
We each must give our all.
Luke 21:1–4

106 In the outward expression of our life together, we
seek independence from the conformist pressures of
Rom 12:1–2; Jas 4:4
consumer culture. Though it appears to offer boundless choice, it is in fact often artificial and hostile to
1 Jn 2:15–17
the growth of true individuality and integrity.

That is why in our manner of dress we reject trends
and fashions, driven as they so often are by status-
seeking and the exploitation of sexuality. Members
dress in a manner that expresses our values of
Matt 6:28–33
simplicity, equality, and modesty, in reverence for
1 Pet 3:1–5; Jas 2:1–8
the way God created man and woman different from
1 Cor 11:2–16
each other yet both in his image.

107 The only sure basis for individual integrity is a
Phil 1:21; Col 3:1–3
living relationship with Christ. Our life together in
church community will wither away unless each of
John 15:1–8
us remains personally connected with him. For this
reason, times of quiet alone before God are important
Mark 1:29–39; Matt 14:22–23
for every brother and sister. Each one has to find the
right rhythm between silence and fellowship, that is,
between encountering God in solitude or through
community with others.

All members must be diligent in taking time for personal prayer mornings and evenings and throughout the day. All must take an active part in seeing that Christ alone is Master among us. Then God will be free *John 14:12–14* to pour out his love on us and the world; then he can *Eph 3:14–21* perform great deeds and "do far more abundantly than all that we ask or think."

The Common Table

108 Our common meals, which we share daily, are an important and joyful part of church community *Acts 2:46; 1 Tim 4:4* life. Each meal is a time of thanksgiving. We often invite visitors, neighbors, friends, and newcomers as guests to our table, whether in our family homes or *Heb 13:1–2; 1 Pet 4:9* communal dining hall; through practicing hospitality as commanded by Scripture, everyone is enriched. When eating together, we celebrate occasions such as birthdays and anniversaries, often with children's performances, music, or other presentations. We observe the major holidays of the church calendar with special festivity: Advent and Christmas, Holy Week and Easter, Ascension Day and Pentecost.

Taken in a spirit of thanksgiving, every mealtime gains deep significance through Jesus' example. He *Mark 2:13–17; Luke 14:12–24* ate and drank with outcasts and sinners, fed the five *John 6:1–15* thousand, and broke bread with his disciples as a sign *John 21:1–14* of friendship. In Scripture he speaks of his wish to be *Rev 3:20* with us in the same way: "Behold, I stand at the door

78

and knock; if any one hears my voice and opens the door, I will come in to him and eat with him, and he with me."

In this way, our common meals can become consecrated festivals of community. They point to the goal of our hope: the coming of the kingdom of God. Jesus spoke of this day as the wedding feast, one to which the *Matt 22:1–14* whole world is invited. As described symbolically in the book of Revelation, this feast will be a vast gathering from every people and nation to celebrate the triumph of the love and justice of God: "Then I heard what *Rev 19:6–7* seemed to be the voice of a great multitude, like the sound of many waters and like the sound of mighty thunder peals, crying,

> Hallelujah!
> For the Lord our God
> the Almighty reigns.
> Let us rejoice and exult
> and give him the glory,
> for the marriage of the Lamb has come."

7

CONCLUSION

We give all honor to God, knowing that our life
together is nothing unless it is filled with his love
and continually renewed by his mercy.

1 Cor 13

As Christ commanded, we await the coming of the
kingdom and desire to hasten it on. Our waiting
cannot be passive or somber. Christ promises that
those who truly expect his kingdom will be filled with
his power and joy. He will help them do away with all
compromise and resignation to the status quo. He will
enable them to live already now in the love and justice
of his coming kingdom.

Matt 24:36—25:46

2 Pet 3:11–13

Phil 4:4–9

Acts 1:6–8

John 16:23–33

1 Jn 5:3–5

Rev 21; Ezek 37

We pray that through Christ what is great and eternal
will take hold of us in such a way that it transforms
all that is small.* Christ's spirit can overwhelm every
person, one after the other, until his kingdom fills

Col 1:9–14; Eph 1:15–23

2 Cor 4:16–18

Heb 12:1–3

Joel 2:28–32

---

* Eberhard Arnold, 20 July 1922.

Is 11:1–9 the whole world. Through him our life together will become not narrower, but broader; not more limited, but more boundless; not more regulated, but more

John 10:10 abundant; not more incapable, but more creative; not more sober, but more enthusiastic; not more faint-

Rom 8:28–39 hearted, but more daring. All this is Christ and his
2 Cor 3:12–18 spirit of freedom.

Rev 22:20 Come soon, Lord Jesus.

Amen. ✝

The Bruderhof can be reached at the following addresses:
Woodcrest, Rifton, New York 12471, USA
Darvell, Robertsbridge, East Sussex, TN32 5DR, England